COGNITIVE STRATEGY INSTRUCTION
that Really Improves Children's Academic Performance

MICHAEL PRESSLEY & ASSOCIATES

Jacquelyn Burkell, Teresa Cariglia-Bull, Linda Lysynchuk,
Jacqueline A. McGoldrick, Brynah Schneider,Barbara L. Snyder,
Sonya Symons, Vera E. Woloshyn

Brookline Books

Copyright © 1990 by Brookline Books

Library of Congress Cataloging-in-Publication Data

Pressley, Michael.
    Cognitive strategy instruction that really improves children's academic
    performances / by Michael
J. Pressley & associates, Jacquelyn Burkell, Teresa Cariglia-Bull, Linda
Lysynchuk, Jacqueline A. McGoldrick, Brynah Schneider, Barbara L.
Snyder, Sonya Symons, Vera E. Woloshyn
      215 p.   cm.
    Includes bibliographical references, index.
    ISBN 0-914797-66-2
    1. Thought and thinking—Study and teaching (Elementary)
2. Cognitive learning. 3. Language arts (Elementary)
4. Mathematics—Study and teaching (Elementary) I. Burkell,
Jacquelyn. II. Title.
LB1590.3.P76   1990
372.13—dc20
                                  90-31832
                                  CIP

Published by
Brookline Books
P.O. Box 1046, Cambridge, MA 02238-1046

Contents

Series Preface

This volume is one in a series of short paperbacks that will be published by Brookline Books on the topic of cognitive strategy instruction. The goal of the series is to provide the very best and most up-to-date information about strategy instruction to the educator community.

Two types of books will be featured in the series:

(a) Most will be written by educational researchers who are doing work that directly relates to school performance. Their work will have been reviewed by the general editor, Michael Pressley, before an invitation to submit a book is delivered to them. The editor will only provide invitations to scholars whose research is sound methodologically and unambiguously relevant to education. One clear goal of the series is to make the very best research on cognitive strategy instruction more readily available to teachers.

(b) A few books will be written by scholars who are supervising outstanding demonstration projects in strategy instruction or who have done outstanding integrative work. A few well-known schools and institutes have received or will receive invitations to contribute. Bibliographic scholars who can provide definitive commentary on how to do strategy instruction or who can provide input about changes in curriculum or educational practices that foster better information processing in children will also appear in the series.

All who are involved with the series already are extremely excited about bridging the gap between the researcher/scholar community and the teaching profession. The contributors to this series are all committed to make high quality work accessible to teaching professionals who can translate research findings into telling educational practices.

Because strategy instruction is particularly appropriate for intellectually handicapped populations and because of the committment of the publisher to provide materials to educators servicing students who experience difficulties in school, the series especially will feature outstanding contributions to the learning disabilities literature. But strategy instruction is highly appropriate for normal learners, especially inner city and minority children. The series will focus on conveying these methods for use with those students. Special education is not the exclusive focus of the series.

It is our strong desire to publish books about a variety of cognitive strategy interventions that are worthwhile for children—handicapped, average, and gifted. Authors who feel they might contribute to this effort should contact Milton Budoff at Brookline Books or Michael Pressley at the College of Education of the University of Maryland, College Park, MD, 20742.

Preface

My students and I have been doing research on various aspects of cognitive strategy instruction for more than a decade. During that time, we have written a number of overview papers as well as reported many empirical studies. In recent years we became especially impressed by the need to communicate to the educator community exactly what is known about cognitive strategy instruction. The need follows from the fact that a large number of commercial ventures have emerged that feature cognitive strategy instruction. Few of these are well validated, although they are widely disseminated and recommended by educator professional associations. Most of these products consist of recommendations to teach a number of strategies, some of which enjoy research support and some of which do not. In addition, most of these products are silent about *how* to teach strategies. A book that separated the wheat from the chaff seemed appropriate, and thus, the current effort. We summarize here what we view as the best validated cognitive strategies for teaching academic content to children in grades 1 through 8 as well as some commentary about how strategy instruction should proceed. We believe the teaching professional who knows the strategies in this volume will be in a better position to teach effective cognitive strategies than the many teachers who have bought expensive strategy instructional kits.

Our perspective is definitely not that cognitive strategy instruction can or should be a "quick fix" for children who are experiencing difficulties in school. Rather, cognitive strategy instruction consists of teaching students procedures that sometimes take a while to master, but are worth acquiring because they reflect the processes that people who are good at academic tasks routinely employ. Moreover, we believe that cognitive strategy instruction is not an "add-on," but rather should be routinely included in ongoing instruction and that the specific strategies that are taught should address academic tasks that children are currently confronting in school. Thus, what is offered here are well validated strategies that fit well with the elementary curriculum. There is an emphasis on long-term and thorough teaching of these procedures rather than quick teaching. Finally, cognitive strategy instruction is not suggested as a substitute for content teaching, but rather a complement to it. Our view is that good thinking consists not only of using the right procedures but coordinating use of effective strategies with a well-developed knowledge base. This model of good thinking is elaborated in the first chapter.

This book was developed between September 1987 and January 1989 at the University of Western Ontario. Author Pressley hung his professional hat there from 1979 to 1989 and all of the student associates were enrolled as graduate students in psychology when they participated in the writing of this book. The student associates earned graduate course credit for their participation in the project, a graduate course that was nominally headed by Pressley. There was a great deal of cooperation and interaction between the contributors as the book was developed. Ultimately particular individuals took responsibility for certain sections of the volume. Thus, each chapter is listed with the names of those associates who were principally responsible for the contribution in their order of impact. Pressley appears as the last author of each, reflecting his role as chief devil's advocate, critic, editor, and the person who kept saying, "It seems to me that there might be some work on . . . Go look in the *Journal of* . . . , maybe between 197? and 198?."

A few others deserve mention for both tangible and intangible support they provided. Carla J. Johnson and Janice A. Kurita of the University of Western Ontario were involved in a major project (independent of this volume) to summarize what is known about reading comprehension strategy instruction. Their thinking and perspectives clearly influenced the direction of chapter 3. We are indebted to many colleagues at a number of universities who provided helpful input about their own projects and patiently answered our inquiries. A partial list includes Lynette Bradley (Oxford), Carol Sue Englert (Michigan State), Jill Fitzgerald (North Carolina), Steve Graham (Maryland), Karen Harris (Maryland), Annemarie S. Palincsar (Michigan State), and Taffy Raphael (Michigan State). We thank the Department of Psychology of the University of Western Ontario for providing the course credit opportunity to permit the completion of this work.

Mike Pressley particularly acknowledges Donna Forrest-Pressley's patience for those occasions when working on chapters for the book prevented getting other things done. Tim Pressley often played quietly in Daddy's home office as MP reworked parts of the manuscript.

We also acknowledge the contributions of the teachers from the Peel Board of Education who commented on the first chapter: Dawn Coulter, Greta Blance, Elaine Jackson, Jack Uchida, Lavar Snyder.

Michael Pressley was supported by an operating grant from the Natural Sciences and Engineering Research Council of Canada during the period when the book was written. The student associates were supported partially by the Natural Sciences and Engineering Research Council of Canada and partially through funds administered by the Faculty of Social Sciences and the Graduate School of the University of Western Ontario.

CHAPTER 1

Introduction to Cognitive Strategy Instruction

Over the past several years, cognitive strategy instruction has emerged as a hot topic in educational research. Nonetheless, strategy instruction has not been incorporated into the curriculum on a large scale (e.g., Applebee, 1984, 1986; Durkin, 1979; Thompson, 1985). This discouraging state of affairs is largely because strategy instruction is not always easy for educators to understand or to implement (Pressley, Goodchild, Fleet, Zajchowski, & Evans, 1989). Even so, recent theory and research should do much to increase the likelihood that strategy instruction will be deployed in classrooms (Pressley, Symons, Snyder, & Cariglia-Bull, 1989; Symons, Snyder, Cariglia-Bull, & Pressley, 1989).

First, new theoretical models of competent thinking are more complete and educationally relevant than their predecessors. Autonomous strategy use is characterized in these models as a complex interaction of many factors, most of which are potentially modifiable through instruction. The complexity of these new models makes them more realistic, which should appeal to educators. Second, educational tasks are also being analyzed carefully so that the processing required to carry them out can be specified. These detailed analyses are an important prerequisite to the development of strategy instruction programs. They also assist in explaining to teachers how strategies match the tasks their students face. Third, more complete models of instruction have emerged as a result of both the current models of good thinking and more detailed knowledge of what constitutes competent performance on specific tasks. These instructional models address the important and modifiable components of the thinking process in general and the relevant aspects of some important instructional tasks (e.g., reading comprehension, problem solving).

In this chapter, we elaborate on the ways that research and theory are contributing to the development of strategy instruction that can be deployed in actual classrooms. We also indicate in this introductory chapter how this volume attempts to bridge the gap between the researcher and educator communities.

Educationally Relevant Models of Competent Thinking

For the most part, the theoretical roots of current models of competent thinking lie in the general information processing approach to cognition. Accordingly, current models assume that people initially register information from the environment in their sensory organs (i.e., the eyes, ears, nose etc.). Some of that information is filtered out (ignored) at the sensory level, while the remainder enters short-term memory (consciousness). Short-term memory has a limited capacity to maintain information and thus its contents must be processed in some way (e.g., rehearsed), or they will fade quickly. If processed, information from short-term memory may transfer into long-term memory. The long-term store contains factual information (i.e., declarative knowledge) as well as information about how to do things (i.e., procedural knowledge) (e.g., Anderson, 1983).

Contemporary models of thinking (e.g., Baron, 1985; Brown, Bransford, Ferrara, & Campione, 1983; Sternberg, 1985) are pertinent to educators because they emphasize the aspects of information processing that can be modified through instruction (i.e., the contents of long-term memory) as opposed to the instructionally unmodifiable "architectural" components (i.e., the sensory organs per se or the neurological elements of short- and long-term memory). According to recent models, for instance, the important features of thinking include strategies (procedural knowledge), knowledge about those strategies and about one's own thinking processes (metacognition), knowledge about the world in general (the knowledge base, e. g., elements of cultural and scientific literacy), motivational beliefs, and overall cognitive style (e.g., Baron, 1985; Borkowski, Carr, Rellinger, & Pressley, in press; Meichenbaum, 1977; Nicholls, in press). These components operate in interaction. Whereas older models of thinking emphasized the "hardware" and/or a few "critical" cognitive processes (e.g., Atkinson & Shiffrin, 1968), these recent conceptualizations address the cognitive, metacognitive, and social-emotional aspects of thinking that both affect classroom functioning and can be altered using instruction. Thus, recent models of thinking are both more complete and more educationally relevant than their predecessors.

The Components of Good Srategy Use

We are partial to one particular description of thinking: the good strategy user model (e.g., Pressley, 1986; Pressley, Borkowski, & Schneider, 1987). According to this framework, a good strategy user is one who possesses a variety of strategies and uses these procedures to meet cognitive challenges. These strategies include "tricks" that aid in the performance of very specific tasks. For example, the name "ROY G. BIV" can be used to remember the order of the colors in the spectrum (i.e., Red, Orange, Yellow, Green, Blue,

Indigo, and Violet). This is an example of a first-letter mnemonic strategy (Morris, 1979). There are also more generally applicable strategies including procedures for reading (e.g., self-questioning, constructing representational images, activating prior knowledge, and rereading difficult-to-understand sections of text), problem solving (e.g., means-ends analysis, working forward), writing (e.g., plan, draft, review, & revise tactics), and memorizing (e.g., repetition; relating to previously acquired, associated material). There are also strategies for regulating and promoting the use of other strategies. These include allocating attention to a task, monitoring performance, and searching for relationships between the present task and others that were previously accomplished via strategic mediation. Some more general strategic processes like monitoring sometimes generate information about whether a particular strategy is facilitating task performance (i.e., metacognitive knowledge). In turn, this knowledge permits decisions about whether to continue with a strategy currently in use or abandon it in favor of a potentially more effective approach.

Strategies are rarely used in isolation. Rather, they are integrated into higher-order sequences that accomplish complex cognitive goals. For example, good reading may begin with previewing, activation of prior knowledge about the topic of a to-be-read text, and self-questioning about what might be presented in the text. These prereading activities are then followed by careful reading, reviewing, and rereading as necessary. General strategies (e.g., self-testing) are used to monitor whether subgoals have been accomplished, prompting the reader to move on when it is appropriate to do so or motivating reprocessing when subgoals have not been met. That is, good strategy users evaluate whether the strategies they are using are producing progress toward goals they have set for themselves.

In addition to knowing how to carry out a strategy, good thinkers also know when and where to use the strategies they know, the benefits that follow from using the procedures, and the amount of effort required to carry out strategies. This metacognitive knowledge about strategies enables the good strategy user to recognize when particular strategies are appropriate and to decide whether the potential benefits of strategy use are worth the costs in terms of effort.

Appropriate motivational beliefs also can facilitate competent thinking. Good strategy users see themselves as able to control their own cognitive performance and, thus, they are motivated to devote effort and attention to strategic processing (Clifford, 1984; McCombs, 1980). Particular cognitive styles can also benefit performance. Good strategy users tend to shield strategic processing from competing behaviors, distractions, and emotions (e.g., Kuhl, 1985). They are neither impulsive nor reflective to the point of inaction, but rather, they are appropriately reflective (Baron, 1985; Meichenbaum, 1977). Although they may experience appropriate anxiety when work is not complete (i.e., enough anxiety to motivate doing the work), they are not highly anxious and certainly not to the point that anxiety disrupts cognition (e.g., Tobias, 1979).

Finally, the nonstrategic knowledge base also plays an important role in competent thinking. Sometimes this knowledge base diminishes the need to execute strategies. For instance, serious baseball fans might watch an inning of the game and remember how every out was made—without exerting any strategic effort. For these fans, the knowledge base is so well developed with respect to baseball that they can readily assimilate new information about the game (e.g., Spilich, Vesonder, Chiesi, & Voss, 1979). On the other hand, baseball fans, most of whom are not specialists in neurology or medicine, would remember the names of the twelve cranial nerves more quickly if they used a mnemonic strategy than if they simply read over a list of the twelve names.

A broad knowledge base is often advantageous because it enables the use of particular strategies. For instance, there is evidence to suggest that the prereading strategy of activating prior knowledge about a topic only improves retention of unfamiliar prose material if the reader possesses a good deal of knowledge about the topic. Child soccer experts, for example, process prose about soccer more effectively when they intentionally activate their knowledge about soccer before reading than when they do not activate this knowledge. The same strategy, however, does not benefit students who know little about soccer (e.g., Hasselhorn & Körkel, 1980).

The Good Strategy User

Although we have discussed the components of good strategy use separately, they operate interactively. When confronted with a task, the good strategy user attends to it and exerts effort toward meeting the goal in the belief that appropriately expended effort will lead to competent performance. For many familiar tasks, the situation automatically elicits appropriate strategic procedures. For example, an experienced journalist may unconsciously use a plan-draft-review-revise sequence of strategies to prepare an article (e.g., Flower & Hayes, 1981), while consciously attending only to the content of the piece that is being written. When faced with not-so-familiar tasks, on the other hand, the good strategy user analyzes the situation and attempts to identify similarities between the current problem and more familiar tasks. A student may notice, for example, that a problem now being tackled is much like the time-distance problems studied in algebra class (Mayer, Larkin, & Kadane, 1984).

When similarities are identified, strategies associated with the previous situation are triggered (e.g., "I'll try to work this out like problems that are solved with distance = speed X time"). An orderly strategic plan is then formed (e.g., identify the distance, speed, and time elements of the problem, and organize them into the d = st equation). Use of the strategy and generation of a solution is facilitated by the knowledge base (e.g., mastery of the basic "math facts"). Next, performance is monitored as the strategy is being executed to determine whether there is progress toward the goal. If the problem is only superficially similar to those encountered previously, the strategies that are generated may be inappropriate (e.g., if there is more than one speed mentioned in the problem at hand and several seem necessary to solve the problem, the inadequacy of the d = st procedure would become obvious). The student might then try to substitute other strategies until one is identified that works (e. g., this is a problem that should be set up as speed X time = speed X time). See Table 1-1 for a summary of these elements of good thinking.

Selection, conscious execution, and monitoring of strategies consume short-term memory capacity (e. g., Baddeley, 1980; Case, 1985; Kahnemann, 1973). Selection, execution, and monitoring of strategies all become more automatic with practice, however, and hence require less capacity with additional experience (e.g., Logan, 1985; Schneider, Dumais, & Shiffrin, 1984). Consider a child who is learning to use reading comprehension strategies. The child might practice procedures such as directing attention to relevant parts of text, self-testing, and summarizing. At first, the use of

Table 1-1
Elements of Good Thinking

Use of efficient strategies to accomplish important tasks.

Knowing when and where to use particular strategies.

Coordination of strategies to accomplish complex goals
(e.g., skilled reading involves a sequence of reading comprehension strategies).

Monitoring use of strategies to determine if progress is being made toward cognitive goals.

Possession of extensive world knowledge, especially about cultural and scientific categories of information that are important to know in order to comprehend events and function competently in contemporary society.

Motivational beliefs that promote good thinking (e.g., believing that it is possible to become a better thinker by learning and using appropriate strategies and acquiring relevant world knowledge).

A cognitive style that supports competent thinking (i.e., appropriately reflective and attentive; not overly anxious).

these strategies may be clumsy, and consume most, if not all, of the child's short-term memory capacity, leaving few cognitive resources (i.e., little consciousness) available for the other demands of reading (e.g., integrating what is being read with prior knowledge). With practice, however, the strategies can be carried out more quickly and efficiently, with much less short-term capacity being consumed in the process. That is, strategy use gets easier and more effective with practice.

Task Analysis of Important Educational Tasks

Many tasks that students commonly encounter in the classroom have been carefully analyzed by educational researchers in order to determine the steps or processes involved in successful performance—that is, the strategies students need to execute to do the task well. This type of research, known as task-analysis, has been carried out in various educational domains such as mathematics (Derry, Hawkes, & Tsai, 1987; Mayer, 1986a), problem-solving (Gick, 1980), reading comprehension (Bereiter & Bird, 1985; Garner, 1987), and writing (Hayes & Flower, 1980; Scardamalia & Bereiter, 1986a, 1986b). Successful writers, for instance, follow a four-step sequence that involves planning the composition, writing a draft, reviewing the draft to determine whether the goals set in the planning stage have been met, and finally, performing revisions. Each step in this general sequence can be broken down further into component processes on the basis of additional task analysis (Englert et al., in press), and the entire cycle or parts of it are repeated a number of times as writing proceeds.

Task-analysis is an important step in the development of new strategies and strategy instruction. This information is necessary to develop maximally efficient strategies. Strategies developed on the basis of task-analysis emphasize the steps that are necessary and sufficient to complete a task successfully. Indeed, many powerful strategies have been derived from task-analytic research (see Gagné, 1985; Mayer, 1986a, 1987), including procedures for vocabulary learning (e.g., Pressley, Levin, & McDaniel, 1987), communication (e.g., Elliott-Faust, Pressley, & Dalecki, 1986), and problem-solving (e.g., Butterfield, 1989). In general, each strategy presented in this book is nothing more than a listing of the processes required to accomplish a particular task efficiently.

OVERVIEW OF THIS VOLUME'S ORGANIZATION

Each of the six succeeding chapters cover a different part of the elementary-school curriculum. Some chapters are longer than others, with length determined by the number of well-studied strategies more than by any other factor. Some of these areas are of greater concern to contemporary researchers than are others. The large number of recent references in the reading comprehension, writing, and mathematics chapters reflects great interest in these areas by contemporary researchers.

Each chapter begins with a conceptual overview. We present this information because of a conviction that the reflective teaching practitioner will want to know why the particular strategies are being proposed. These short reviews are not meant to substitute for more in-depth treatments of the issues. The reference list for each chapter directs interested readers to more extensive coverage of the topics, with references placed at the end of the chapter (rather than having a composite list for the entire volume). We did this to provide reading lists of what we regard as the best available strategy-instructional research for each of the six instructional areas covered in the book—decoding, reading comprehension, vocabulary learning, spelling, written composition, and mathematics.

Review of relevant strategies follows the brief conceptual commentary. Three types of strategies are presented in this book. Some strategies are principally ones that teachers can use in presenting material. Thus, presenting mnemonic pictures to aid memory of letter-sound associations is a teaching strategy. So is a type of decoding instruction that is conveyed with a computer program. Each will be identified with a [T] when it is first introduced into the text. Then there are strategies that students could acquire and use on their own. Teaching students a procedure to increase memory of vocabulary, a procedure which they can carry out on their own, is one example of this type of strategy. Each of these, designated as a strategy that can be student self-regulated, will be identified with an [SSR] when first presented in the text. Those strategies that teachers can use to improve their presentations and which eventually can lead to student self-regulated strategy use are marked [T & SSR]. One example would be writing instruction that begins with a teacher providing prompts to improve writing and leads to students eventually prompting themselves.

Student self-regulated strategies are particularly important, but must be taught in a particular way if students are eventually to control the procedures. How to teach such strategies so that students eventually do self-regulate their use of them is becoming better understood, and is covered in detail in the next section.

Teaching SSRs So That Students Eventually Use the Strategies in a Self-Regulated Fashion

Both researchers and educators are studying the issue of *how* to teach strategies most effectively in order to increase the likelihood that students will use strategies autonomously, that is, in a self-regulated fashion. Recent interest in this issue has led to the emergence of several new models of instruction, including the good strategy user perspective on instruction

(Pressley, 1986), the Kansas strategy intervention model (Deshler, Schumaker, & Lenz, 1984; Deshler & Schumaker, in press), direct explanation (e.g., Duffy & Roehler, 1986, 1987; Duffy, Roehler, & Putnam, 1987), and the training arithmetic problem-solving skills model (TAPS) (e.g., Derry, et al., 1987). The first two examples are general prescriptions for instruction across domains, whereas the second two address strategy instruction within the domains of reading and mathematical problem-solving respectively.

While these models differ superficially with respect to terminology and emphasis, they also have many similarities. Rather than review each one in detail, we have chosen to focus on commonalities. In general, there is a common pedagogical perspective in these models: All of the components of good strategy use receive instructional attention. That is, metacognitive information about strategies (e.g., when and where to use them), nonstrategic knowledge, and appropriate motivational beliefs are imparted as strategies are taught.

Strategies

Recent instructional prescriptions suggest that students should be taught effective strategies that are well-matched to the actual tasks that are presented in school. Current models favor teaching only a few strategies at a time and teaching them well, as opposed to teaching many strategies concurrently and superficially. New strategies are introduced once old ones are well known. Strategy instruction is perceived as a long-term endeavor because the learning of individual strategies takes time (more later in this chapter about this) and there are a number of important strategies that can be taught (Pressley et al., 1989), although a main theme of this volume is that the number is not insurmountable.

Monitoring

Recent models of strategy instruction emphasize that students should be taught to monitor how they are doing. As students execute strategies, they should be taught to check performance in order to keep track of their progress. They should also be encouraged to try to remediate any problems they experience. On-line checking of cognitive progress needs to be taught since even good students sometimes fail to monitor performance adequately and/or fail to take corrective measures when problems are spotted (e.g., Garner, 1987; Markman, 1981; Schneider & Pressley, 1989, Chapter 7).

Metacognition about Strategies

Making certain that students know when and where to use strategies is another important aspect of strategy instruction. This information may be explained to students directly, or it may be abstracted by students during extensive practice across settings where strategies can be employed. The former tactic is preferable since children are not efficient at discovering metacognitive information on their own (Pressley, Borkowski, & O'Sullivan, 1984, 1985; Pressley, Levin, & Ghatala, 1984), nor do they automatically apply it even if it is independently discovered (e.g., Pressley, Ross, Levin, & Ghatala, 1984). Abstracting metacognitive information during strategy practice is more likely to work if students are taught methods for noting when and whether the strategies they are using work (e.g., if they are taught to compare how they do with a strategy versus how they do when not using the strategy) (Pressley, Borkowski, & O'Sullivan, 1984).

It is necessary to impart metacognitive information about strategies because of the critical role it plays in the generalization and maintenance of strategies. In order to deploy strategies broadly and appropriately, students must possess knowledge about when and where strategies should be used—that is, teaching metacognitive information about strategies boils down largely to making certain that students know when the strategies they are learning should be deployed.

Student Motivation

Students are most likely to be motivated to use strategies if they are aware that strategic procedures do in fact enhance performance (e.g., Brown et al., 1983). Thus, strategy instruction should include explicit information about the utility of the strategies being taught. Explanations as to how strategies can be helpful, feedback about strategy-mediated performance, and having students chart their progress while using strategies may all serve to increase motivation.

In a more global sense, children also need to be made aware that competent functioning is often a result of using appropriate strategies rather than superior innate ability or just trying hard (Pressley et al., 1989). Students should be taught that they can become competent thinkers by employing the strategies used by successful learners. It should be emphasized to students that strategies are processes that resemble what really good students do when they tackle tasks in school. Students who believe that they can become more intellectually competent by learning the procedures used by competent people should have high motivation to learn the strategies described in later chapters of this book.

Styles

Students need to be encouraged to adopt a general intellectual style that is consistent with good strategy use. The instructional setting should promote a comfortable, reflective pace and calm academic activity rather than anxiety. When given an academic task, students need to know that it is appropriate to reflect upon what is required in that particular situation. Make students aware of the need to shield themselves from distractions when doing academic work. Let them know the importance of attention to tasks and encourage appropriate attention.

Teaching in Context

Strategies should not be taught as a separate topic in the curriculum. Rather, they should be taught throughout the curriculum as part of the actual academic tasks that students encounter. Important strategies are best learned when they are practiced with the kinds of materials that students are expected to master when using the strategies. Thus, when students are given a writing assignment as part of a social studies unit, this is an opportunity to teach strategic procedures for producing high quality written compositions.

Interactions Between Strategies and the Knowledge Base

The teaching of strategies alone is not sufficient. The competent thinker possesses many pieces of knowledge, and strategy use is often dependent on this knowledge. Successful performance is not attributable to either strategies or knowledge independently (e.g., Glaser, 1984) but rather, to strategies and nonstrategic knowledge operating together. Thus, instructional attention should be given to expanding the student's knowledge base in addition to expanding his or her repertoire of strategies. But if students master effective strategies (e.g., reading comprehension strategies), it should be easier for them to learn more and to do so more efficiently than they would otherwise. Thus, strategy instruction can promote the goal of content learning and is in no way antagonistic to it.

Interactive Direct Teaching

Contemporary models of instruction advocate direct explanation and/or modeling of strategic procedures. There is gradual releasing of control from the teacher to the student, with teachers resuming greater control as needed. Thus, teachers describe and model strategies initially, and then allow a great deal of student practice in order for students to master those strategies. This practice is monitored by the teacher, who provides individually tailored corrective feedback and encouragement. It is to be expected that mastery of a strategy will take some time and a lot of re-explanations. Generalization of strategies is promoted by explicitly providing guidance and reminders to students about when and how strategies can be extended to new situations. This direct explanation approach contrasts with alternative models that view the teacher as someone who should explain procedures briefly and then assign unsupervised practice, or as someone who should supervise discovery learning procedures (e.g., Brainerd, 1978; Pressley, Snyder, & Cariglia-Bull, 1987).

Summary

A general outline of how to teach a strategy can be drawn from the common pedagogical perspective of current instructional models (Pressley et al., 1988). The first step in teaching a strategy is to describe the strategy to students. This can be accomplished by the teacher modeling actual use of the strategy, particularly with "thinking aloud" statements about how to execute the procedure. Descriptions of the strategy include important metacognitive information such as why the strategy should be used, what it accomplishes, and specific situations in which the strategy is applicable.

Once students know the steps that comprise a strategy, they should be given plenty of guided practice, during which the teacher provides reinforcement as well as feedback about how to improve execution of the strategy. Practice should begin with fairly simple materials and progress to grade-appropriate work. Because instruction is given until students can execute the strategy proficiently, there is a great deal of responsibility on the teacher to monitor student progress, diagnose student difficulties, and adjust instruction accordingly.

Strategy generalization is encouraged by having students practice strategies with different types of materials (e.g., a summarizing strategy could be practiced with social studies, science, and general interest articles). Strategy use is also prompted during the course of the school day when situations arise in which the procedure can be used. Students should be taught to be alert for cues in the instructional environment indicating that a strategy might apply. Throughout instruction, the teacher emphasizes the utility of the strategy itself as well as the importance of strategy use in general.

Strategy instruction should be explicit, intensive, and extensive. The ultimate goal is to have students using the trained strategies autonomously, skillfully, and appropriately. Strategies should be taught to students directly over an extended period of time as part of the existing curriculum. Other components of effective thinking such as metacognition, motivation, and the nonstrategic knowledge base must also be addressed by instruction. That is, students are provided input about when and where to use the strategies they are learning; they are shown how their performance improves by using the right strategies, with a lot of emphasis on the theme that learning how to do important tasks is a critical part of intellectual development. Teaching of important content is not sacrificed in order to teach strategies, but rather teaching of strategies is integrated with teaching of content. By attending to both the strategic and nonstrategic elements of competent performance, contemporary models of strategy instruction are more complete than previous ones, which emphasized brief instruction of strategies and focussed only on teaching the steps required to carry out the strategic procedures. The most important teaching recommendations are summarized in Table 1-2.

Table 1-2
General Model of How to Teach Strategies

Teach a few strategies at a time, intensively and extensively, as part of the ongoing curriculum.

Model and explain new strategies.

Model again and re-explain strategies in ways that are sensitive to aspects of strategy use that are not well understood.

Explain to student where and when to use strategies.

Provide plenty of practice, using strategies for as many appropriate tasks as possible.

Encourage students to monitor how they are doing when they are using strategies.

Encourage continued use of and generalization of strategies.

Increase students' motivation to use strategies by heightening student awareness that they are acquiring valuable skills that are at the heart of competent functioning.

Emphasize reflective processing rather than speedy processing; do all possible to eliminate high anxiety in students; encourage students to shield themselves from distraction so they can attend to academic tasks.

CLOSING THE GAP BETWEEN RESEARCH AND PRACTICE

Strategy instruction that addresses the elements of good strategy use is clearly not a simple matter. It is a long-term endeavor that cuts across all areas of the school curriculum. Thus, widespread practice of strategy instruction may require changes in teacher training, instructional methods, and the current curriculum (Pressley et al., 1989). Given these obstacles to implementation, it is not very surprising that strategy instruction is not widespread at this point in time. It is our perspective, however, that changes in the ways that information about strategy instruction is disseminated may increase teachers' abilities and willingness to teach strategies. That was the greatest motivation for writing this book!

Pressley and his colleagues (Pressley et al., 1989) identify a number of obstacles to the dissemination of information about strategies and strategy instruction. These include the large number of strategies, the lack of evaluation data for many strategies, and the inaccessability to practitioners of existing research that is normally published in academic journals. Essentially, these obstacles boil down to poor communications between researchers and those for whom their work has direct implications. Unless information produced in educational research is available, manageable, and appealing to practitioners, it will have no impact. We feel that researchers would do well to create a positive regard for strategy instruction on the part of educators. To this end, researchers must demonstrate they have something concrete to offer in the way of effective, teachable strategies.

The current instructional literature is filled with strategy suggestions (e.g., Chipman, Segal, & Glaser, 1985; Segal, Chipman, & Glaser, 1985; Nickerson, Perkins, & Smith, 1985). Such a large volume of strategies would be overwhelming if a teacher had to to teach all or most of them. Moreover, the literature would be difficult to sort through for someone who wishes to select only a few strategies to present in the classroom. This state of affairs may discourage educator interest from the very beginning, and does little to encourage a positive regard for strategy instruction.

To complicate matters, many of the strategies that are advocated in the curriculum literature have not been adequately evaluated. Often, strategies are promoted on the basis of meagre evidence or their theoretical and intuitive appeal (Mayer, 1986b; Pressley, Cariglia-Bull, & Snyder, 1984). Some strategies are offered commercially and adapted by educators only because they "seem like they should work" or they "sound good." This is a serious problem because resources are wasted when the strategies that are taught are ineffective or, worse yet, harmful to students. In addition, when educators recognize that a strategy does not lead to the gains it was supposed to produce, there may be a sense that all of strategy instruction is a hoax. In short, it is a real challenge for educators to obtain sufficient information to separate strategies that have not been evaluated from those that have been tested, and then to separate the ones that produce important educational gains from those that do not. *This book should alleviate some of the problems related to the dissemination of information about strategies.*

Specifically, we have identified teachable strategies for many areas of the elementary school curriculum. Most strategies presented here have been tested in true experiments (Campbell & Stanley, 1966). A few, however, have yet to prove their worth in true experiments, either because the validation studies have not been completed at the time of this writing, or they were evaluated in a nonexperimental fashion. In every case, however, there is at least some data-based analysis suggesting the method improves student performance, though in a few cases uncontrolled pretest-posttest designs were used so that whether strategy instruction is causing the performance gains cannot be determined with confidence. (Strategies not yet evaluated in true experiments will be cited as such when they are presented.) This book is not an exhaustive catalogue of strategies that can be taught to children, but rather, a selective presentation of procedures that have the most evidence to support their use with elementary school-age children.

This book contains a small, but well-substantiated, list of strategies that any teacher of elementary children can use to begin a strategy instruction program encompassing many areas of the curriculum. Most of the strategies are ones that many students can learn to execute on their own (i.e., they have the potential to become student self-regulated strategies [SSRs]). These strategies should be taught according to the guidelines for instruction presented earlier in this chapter.

We reiterate the strong recommendation to try teaching only a few strategies at a time, to model and to explain those few strategies a lot, to reexplain them as necessary, and to be prepared to do a lot of reexplanation. Make certain that students know when and where to use the strategies that they learn.

Teaching strategies in the context of social studies, science, and literary tasks that children are expected to accomplish as part of the elementary curriculum increases the likelihood children will learn the applicability of strategies to actual educational tasks.

Although a clear focus of this volume is the development of students who know and use strategies, we are also including teaching strategies (the [T] strategies) because they complement well the main goal of teaching students to use strategies: Teaching students to execute effective strategies makes good student performance more likely; so should the use of teaching strategies. In summary, there are a lot of suggestions in this volume for improving student performance on academic tasks, including both ways of increasing students' self-directed use of efficient processing and ways of improving teachers' presentation of materials.

REFERENCES

Anderson, J.R. (1983). *The architecture of cognition*. Cambridge, MA: Harvard University Press.

Applebee, A.N. (1984). *Contexts for learning to write*. Norwood, NJ: Ablex.

Applebee, A.N. (1986). Problems in process approaches: Toward a reconceptualization of process instruction. In A.R. Petrosky, P. Bartholomae, & K.J. Rehage (Eds.), *The teaching of writing; Eighty-fifth Yearbook of the National Society for the Study of Education* (pp. 95-113). Chicago: University of Chicago Press.

Atkinson, R.C., & Shiffrin, R.M. (1968). Human memory: A proposed system and its control processes. In W. Spence & J.T. Spence (Eds.), *The psychology of learning and motivation* (Vol. 2). New York: Academic Press.

Baddeley, A. (1980). *Working memory*. New York: Oxford University Press.

Baron, J. (1985). *Rationality and intelligence*. Cambridge, England: Cambridge University Press.

Bereiter, C., & Bird, M. (1985). Use of thinking aloud in identification and teaching of reading comprehension strategies. *Cognition and Instruction, 2*, 91-130.

Borkowski, J.G., Carr, M., Rellinger, E., & Pressley, M. (in press). Self-regulated cognition: Interdependence of metacognition, attributions, and self-esteem. In B.F. Jones & L. Idol (Eds.), *Dimensions of thinking and cognitive instruction*. Hillsdale, NJ: Lawrence Erlbaum Associates.

Brainerd, C.J. (1978). Learning research and Piagetian theory. In L.S. Siegel & C.J. Brainerd (Eds.), *Alternatives to Piaget: Critical essays on the theory* (pp. 69- 109). New York: Academic Press.

Brown, A.L., Bransford, J.P., Ferrara, R.A., & Campione, J.C. (1983). Learning, remembering, and understanding. In J.H. Flavell & E.M. Markman (Eds.), *Handbook of child psychology: vol. 3. Cognitive development* (pp. 177-206). New York: John Wiley & Sons.

Butterfield, E. C. (1989). On solving the transfer problem. In M. Gruneberg, M., Sykes, R.N., & Morris, P.E. (Eds.), *Proceedings of the second conference on the practical aspects of memory*. London: John Wiley & Sons.

Campbell, P.T., & Stanley, J.C. (1966). *Experimental and quasiexperimental designs for research.* Chicago: Rand McNally.

Case, R. (1985). *Intellectual development.* Orlando, FL: Academic Press.

Chipman, S F., Segal, J.W., & Glaser, R. (Eds.) (1985). *Thinking and learning skills: Vol. 2. Research and open questions.* Hillsdale, NJ: Lawrence Erlbaum Associates.

Clifford, M.M. (1984). Thoughts on a theory of constructive failure. *Educational Psychologist, 19,* 108-120.

Derry, S.J., Hawkes, L.W., & Tsai, C-J. (1987). A theory for remediating problem-solving skills of older children and adults. *Educational Psychologist, 22,* 55-87.

Deshler, P.P., & Schumaker, J.B. (in press). An instructional model for teaching students how to learn. In J.L. Graden, J.E. Zins, & M.J. Curtis (Eds.), *Alternative educational delivery systems: Enhancing instructioral options for all students.*

Deshler, D.P., Schumaker, J.B., & Lenz, B.K. (1984). Academic and cognitive interventions for LD adolescents (Part I). *Journal of Learning Disabilities, 17,* 108-117.

Duffy, G.G., & Roehler, L.R. (1986). *Improving classroom reading instruction: A decision-making approach.* New York: Random House.

Duffy, G.G., & Roehler, L.R. (1987). Improving reading instruction through the use of responsive elaboration. *The Reading Teacher, 40,* 514-520.

Duffy, G.G., Roehler, L.R., & Putnam, J. (1987). Putting the teacher in control: Basal textbooks and teacher decision making. *Elementary School Journal, 87,* 357-366.

Durkin, D. (1979). What classroom observations reveal about reading comprehension instruction. *Reading Research Quarterly, 14,* 481-538.

Elliott-Faust, D.J., Pressley, M., & Dalecki, L.B. (1986). Process training to improve children's referential communication: Asher and Wigfield (1981) revisited. *Journal of Educational Psychology, 78,* 22-26.

Englert, C.S., Raphael, T.E., Anderson, L.M., Anthony, H., Fear, K., & Gregg, S. (in press). A case for writing instruction: Strategies for writing informational text. *Learning Disabilities Focus.*

Flower, L.S., & Hayes, J.R. (1981). A cognitive process theory of writing. *College Composition and Communication, 32,* 305-387.

Gagné, E.D. (1985). *The cognitive psychology of school learning.* Boston: Little, Brown, & Co.

Garner, R. (1987). *Metacognition and reading comprehension.* Norwood, NJ: Ablex.

Gick, M. L. (1980). Problem-solving strategies. *Educational Psychologist, 21,* 99-120.

Glaser, R. (1984). Education and thinking: The role of knowledge. *American Psychologist, 39,* 93-104.

Hasselhorn, M., & Körkel, J. (1980). Metacognitive versus traditional reading instructions: The mediating role of domain-specific knowledge on children's text processing. *Human Learning, 5,* 75-90.

Hayes, J.R., & Flower, L.S. (1980). Identifying the organization of writing processes. In L.W. Gregg & E.R. Steinberg (Eds.), *Cognitive processes in writing* (pp. 3-30). Hillsdale, NJ: Lawrence Erlbaum Associates.

Kahnemann, P. (1973). *Attention and effort.* Englewood Cliffs, NJ: Prentice Hall.

Kuhl, J. (1985). Volitional mediators of cognition-behavior consistency: Self-regulatory processes and action control versus state orientation. In J. Kuhl & J. Beckmann (Eds.), *Action control: From cognition to behavior* (pp. 101-128). New York: Springer-Verlag.

Logan, G.P. (1985). Skill and automaticity: Relations, implications, and future directions. *Canadian Journal of Psychology, 39,* 367-386.

Markman, E.M. (1981). Comprehension monitoring. In W.P. Dickson (Ed.), *Children's oral communication skills* (pp. 61-84). New York: Academic Press.

Mayer, R.E. (1986a). Mathematics. In R.F. Dillon & R.J. Sternberg (Eds.), *Cognition and instruction* (pp. 127-154). Orlando FL: Academic Press.

Mayer, R.E. (1986b). Teaching students how to think and learn: A look at some instructional programs and the research: A review of J.W. Segal, S.F. Chipman, & R. Glaser's (1985) *Thinking and learning skills: Vol. 1. Relating instruction to research* and S.F. Chipman, J.W. Segal, &

R. Glaser's (1985) *Thinking and learning skills: Vol. 2. Research and open questions. Contemporary Psychology, 31* 753-756.

Mayer, R.E. (1987). *Educational psychology: A cognitive approach.* Boston, MA: Little, Brown, & Co.

Mayer, R.E., Larkin, J.H., & Kadane, J. (1984). A cognitive analysis of mathematical problem solving ability. In R. Sternberg (Ed.), *Advances in the psychology of human intelligence,* (Vol. 2, pp. 231-273). Hillsdale, NJ: Lawrence Erlbaum Associates.

McCombs, B.L. (1986). The role of the self-system in self-regulated learning. *Contemporary Educational Psychology, 11,* 314-332.

Meichenbaum, P.M. (1977). *Cognitive behavior modification.* New York: Plenum.

Morris, P.E. (1979). Strategies for learning and recall. In M.M. Gruneberg & P.E. Morris (Eds.), *Applied problems in memory* (pp. 25-57). London: Academic Press.

Nicholls, J.G. (in press). What is ability and why are we mindful of it? A developmental perspective. In J. Kolligian, Jr., & R J. Sternberg (Eds.), *Perceptions of competence and incompetence across the lifespan.* New Haven, CT: Yale University Press.

Nickerson, R.S., Perkins, D.N., & Smith, E.E. (Eds.), (1985). *The teaching of thinking.* Hillsdale, NJ: Lawrence Erlbaum Associates.

Pressley, M. (1986). The relevance of the good strategy user model to the teaching of mathematics. *Educational Psychologist, 21,* 139-161.

Pressley, M., Borkowski, J.G., & O'Sullivan, J.T. (1984). Memory strategy instruction is made of this: Metamemory and durable strategy use. *Educational Psychologist, 19,* 94-107.

Pressley, M., Borkowski, J.G., & O'Sullivan, J.T. (1985). Children's metamemory and the teaching of memory strategies. In D.L. Forrest-Pressley, G.E. MacKinnon, & T.G. Waller (Eds.), *Metacognition, cognition, and human performance* (pp. 111-153). Orlando, FL: Academic Press.

Pressley, M., Borkowski, J.G., & Schneider, W. (1987). Cognitive strategies: Good strategy users coordinate metacognition and knowledge. In R. Vasta & G. Whitehurst (Eds.), *Annals of Child Development* (Vol. 5, pp. 89-129). New York: JAI Press.

Pressley, M., Cariglia-Bull, T., & Snyder, B.L. (1984). Are there programs that can really teach thinking and learning skills: A review of Segal, Chipman, & Glaser's *Thinking and learning skills: Vol. 1. Relating instruction to research. Contemporary Education Review, 3,* 435-444.

Pressley, M., Goodchild, F., Fleet, J., Zajchowski, R., & Evans, E.D. (1989). The challenges of classroom strategy instruction. *Elementary School Journal, 89,* 301-342.

Pressley, M., Johnson, C.J., Symons, S.E., McGoldrick, J., Kurita, J., & Pressley, M. (1988). *Reading comprehension strategies that can be taught efficiently.* Manuscript submitted for publication. London, Ontario: Department of Psychology, University of Western Ontario.

Pressley, M., Levin, J.R., & Ghatala, E.S. (1984). Memory strategy monitoring in adults and children. *Journal of Verbal Learning and Verbal Behavior, 23,* 270-288.

Pressley, M., Levin, J.R., & McDaniel, M.A. (1987). Remembering versus inferring what a word means: Mnemonic and contextual approaches. In M. McKeown & M.E. Curtis (Eds.), *The nature of vocabulary acquisition* (pp. 107-127). Hillsdale, NJ: Lawrence Erlbaum Associates.

Pressley, M., Ross, K.A., Levin, J.R., & Ghatala, E.S. (1984). The role of strategy utility knowledge in children's strategy decision making. *Journal of Experimental Child Psychology, 38,* 491-504.

Pressley, M., Snyder, B.L., & Cariglia-Bull, T. (1987). How can good strategy use be taught to children?: Evaluation of six alternative approaches. In S. Cormier & J. Hagman (Eds.), *Transfer of learning: Contemporary research and applications* (pp. 81-121). Orlando, FL: Academic Press.

Pressley, M., Symons, S.E., Snyder, B.L., & Cariglia-Bull, T. (1989). Strategy instruction research is coming of age. *Learning Disabilities Quarterly, 12,* 16-30.

Scardamalia, M., & Bereiter, C. (1986a). Research on written composition. In M.C. Wittrock (Ed.), *Handbook of research on teaching.* New York: Macmillan.

Scardamalia, M., & Bereiter, C. (1986b). Writing. In R.F. Dillon & R.J. Sternberg (Eds.), *Cognition and instruction* (pp. 59-81). Orlando, FL: Academic Press.

Schneider, W., Dumais, S.T., & Shiffrin, R.M. (1984). Automatic and control processing and attention. In R. Parasuraman & D.R. Davies (Eds.), *Varieties of attention* (pp. 1-27). Orlando, FL: Academic Press.

Schneider, W., & Pressley, M. (1989). *Memory development between 2 and 20*. New York & Berlin: Springer-Verlag.

Segal, J.W., Chipman, S.F., & Glaser, R. (Eds.) (1985). *Thinking and learning skills: Vol. 1. Relating research to instruction*. Hillsdale, NJ:Lawrence Erlbaum Associates.

Spilich, G.J., Vesonder, G.T., Chiesi, H.L., & Voss, J.F. (1979). Text processing of domain-related information for individuals with high and low domain knowledge. *Journal of Verbal Learning and Verbal Behavior, 18*, 275-290.

Sternberg, R.J. (1985). *Beyond IQ: A triarchic theory of human intelligence*. London & New York: Cambridge University Press.

Symons, S.E., Snyder, B.L., Cariglia-Bull, T., & Pressley, M. (1989). Why be optimistic about cognitive strategy instruction? In C.B. McCormick, G.E. Miller, & M. Pressley (Eds.), *Cognitive strategy research: From basic research to educational applications*. New York & Berlin: Springer-Verlag.

Thompson, A.G. (1985). Teachers' conceptions of mathematics and the teaching of problem solving. In E.A. Silver (Ed.), *Teaching and learning mathematical problem solving* (pp. 281-294). Hillsdale, NJ: Lawrence Erlbaum Associates.

Tobias, S. (1979). Anxiety research in educational psychology. *Journal of Educational Psychology, 71*, 573-582.

CHAPTER 2

Decoding

Decoding involves "making sense" out of printed words. It involves learning to discriminate letters from each other, as well as identifying letters and letter clusters. In order to decode successfully, a child must understand how symbols relate to sounds. Word decoding is an important component of early reading skill (Calfee, Lindamood & Lindamood, 1973; Curtis, 1980; Just & Carpenter, 1987; Perfetti & Hogaboam, 1975; Torgeson, 1986), and for most children, decoding is the major skill to be learned during early reading instruction (Just & Carpenter, 1987).

Current theories of reading stress the interactive nature of the components of reading: reading is an information-processing task which changes according to the skills of the reader (Underwood, 1985). According to Perfetti's verbal efficiency theory, decoding skills must be automatic, so that the execution of this process of reading will not require much attentional capacity. By reducing the amount of capacity required for the execution of the decoding process, more capacity is made available for the execution of other higher-order processes, such as comprehension (Lesgold & Perfetti, 1981; Perfetti, Finger & Hogaboam, 1978; Perfetti & Hogaboam, 1975; Perfetti & Roth, 1981).

Whole-Word or Phonics?

Most educators would agree that decoding skills are important in reading. However, there is little consensus with respect to how these skills should be taught. Two historically opposed views to reading instruction are the whole-word and phonics approaches. Whole-word programs stress the importance of reading for meaning and enjoyment (Beck, 1981). Children learn to read words by looking at their global shape. To remember a word, the child is encouraged to think of the meaning of the word while looking at it. There is little emphasis on the specific letters that make up the word. Contextual cues are to be used to recognize unknown words. With continued practice, the child develops his or her sight word vocabulary (Beck, 1981; Just & Carpenter, 1987). In contrast, the phonics approach emphasizes the teaching of symbol-sound correspondences. Phonics instruction precedes the reading lesson: the to-be-read story is made up of words that can be decoded using the phonics skills taught up to that point (Beck, 1981).

Despite unambiguous theoretical distinctions between the two approaches, many programs used today cannot be defined as solely "phonics" or "whole-word": most programs incorporate aspects of both, and it becomes a difference in emphasis (Barr, 1984; Beck, 1981). For example, some programs which emphasize reading for meaning may include a short phonics lesson as a supplement to instruction. Conversely, many phonics-emphasis programs also encourage reading for meaning. Beck (1981) suggests that the difference between the two approaches has dwindled to a difference in the timing of letter-sound instruction: phonics approaches teach these correspondences early in instruction, whereas whole-word programs tend to delay this aspect of instruction until later years of schooling.

In early reading programs, decoding instruction has two main goals: first, children must learn to recognize certain words on sight (i.e., they have to develop an adequate sight word vocabulary); second, children must learn the techniques necessary to decode new words (Just & Carpenter, 1987).

Poor readers have deficient decoding skills. For example, the good reader-poor reader distinction is maximized in situations that rely heavily on decoding skill—that is, in situations involving pseudowords and low frequency words (i.e. Perfetti & Hogaboam, 1975). Good readers are able to rely on their knowledge of letter-sound patterns, whereas for poor readers, "code-breaking" is a slow and laborious process (Perfetti & Hogaboam, 1975). Good readers are able to decode on the basis of multiletter units (i.e. -tion, -ing, -ance) that have fairly simple pronunciation rules and can be carried out quickly. In contrast, poor readers decode letter-by-letter, which involves more complex rules and results in slower decoding (Frederiksen, 1981). Thus, it makes sense that interventions should be aimed at improving word attack skills.

Both whole-word and phonics programs have their strengths and weaknesses, and there have been many attempts to determine the "superior method" of instruction. In general, phonics instruction has proven to be superior to the whole-word method with respect to word attack skills (Barr, 1984; Beck, 1981; Gettinger, 1981; Johnson & Baumann, 1984; Just & Carpenter, 1987; Pflaum, Walberg, Karegianes & Rasher, 1980; Vellutino & Scanlon, 1986). Children seem to need to be taught directly the relations between letters and sounds in order to become good, independent readers (Bradley, 1987: Ehri & Wilce, 1983). Early, fairly intensive phonics instruction helps produce readers that are able to pronounce new words accurately (Johnson & Baumann, 1984).

Gettinger (1986) compared the effectiveness of the whole-word and phonics approaches and produced typical results. She found that although the whole-word approach resulted in slightly better performance on trained words, the phonics approach produced far superior performance on transfer words. Imagine how difficult the task of learning to read would be to a child if he/she had to be taught how to read each and every word. Awareness of the relation between graphemes and phonemes encourages the child to be more discriminating in his/her processing of printed words and facilitates the detection of letter-sound patterns which will make learning new words easier (Vellutino & Scanlon, 1986).

Taylor and Taylor (1983) summarized this point in their review of the literature:

> Phonics is necessary for secure decoding of many new words. And it cannot be left entirely to children to induce by themselves, for not all children are bright and not all materials are optimal for induction (p.384).

Systematic instruction in phonics provides a child with the skills necessary to become an independent reader at an early age (Taylor & Taylor, 1983).

The following section introduces strategies that can be used to teach decoding. The list is by no means exhaustive: the strategies chosen for presentation are those which have received at least some empirical support.

STRATEGIES TO TEACH DECODING

The Method of Repeated Readings [T]

LaBerge and Samuels (1974) argue that basic processes in reading, such as decoding, must be automatic before more indepth processing, such as comprehension, can occur. A fluent reader decodes text automatically, and therefore can devote his/her attention to comprehending what is read (LaBerge & Samuels, 1974). A beginning reader devotes his/her attention to decoding, and therefore cannot devote attention to the comprehension of what is read. For the beginning reader, then, the process of what is read is much more slow and laborious (Samuels, 1979). This theory parallels the verbal efficiency theory put forth by Perfetti and Lesgold (1977), which also states that underlying processes must be conducted efficiently in order for there to be sufficient residual processing capacity for comprehension to take place. Theories such as these stress the importance of good decoding skills. In order to achieve automaticity in decoding, a lot of practice is required. A cost-efficient way of providing extensive practice is through the method of repeated readings.

The method of repeated readings can be easily implemented in any classroom. It simply involves having a child repeatedly read a short, meaningful passage until a predetermined level of fluency is reached. Fluency is defined by the accuracy of word recognition as well as reading speed (Samuels, 1979). Once fluency is achieved, the procedure is repeated with a new passage. The passages increase in length as the child's reading skills improve. As the number of passages successfully read increases, fewer rereadings are required before the criterion fluency level is reached. Practice with many passages is more effective than practice with only one story (Dowhower, 1987). Keeping a graph of individual reading scores is usually a good idea, since it makes obvious to the child that he or she is making progress in reading, which should affect motivation positively.

The method of repeated readings can be conducted with or without audio support. Children begin the training by reading a passage along with a tape recording. The audio support is gradually removed with progressive readings. Dowhower (1987) suggests that audio support be used for extremely slow readers (under 45 words per minute), since it reduces the amount of monitoring and encouragement these readers require. She claims that after one or two error-free readings with the tape recording, these children are ready to read without audio support.

The method of repeated readings is an appealing method of instruction, since it can be used with the materials already available in any classroom. It is adaptable to virtually any reading material, as long as the passages chosen are short at first and then increase in length as training progresses. The method is meant to be an adjunct to the regular reading curriculum; it is not meant to replace direct reading instruction (Samuels, 1979). While the teacher is instructing one group of children, the remaining children can be practicing repeated reading, either on their own or with the help of other students. It can be used with tutors, peer partners or teachers' aides (Dowhower, 1987), whose role is to provide feedback and encouragement (Carver & Hoffman, 1981).

Adaptations of This Method

This method has also been attempted using phrases and lists of words during training (Fleisher, Jenkins and Pany 1979). The 30-minute training sessions involve one-to-one instruction and testing. Each child is given a flash card drill on the words from a 100-word passage. The order of the words in the list is random on each trial, and practice is terminated after the child is able to read the list of words at a rate of 90 wpm or faster. When the child has mastered the list of words, he or she is presented with a story that is made up of the same words. The child is then required to read the story out loud, and it is stressed that the child is to read for understanding.

A similar procedure is used when training phrases: the child is given repeated practice on reading phrases from the story until the fluency criterion is reached, that is, the child is reading at a rate of 160 words per minute without error. The child is then allowed to read the story from which the trained phrases were extracted.

Caution is warranted in using the method of repeated readings, since the effects do not generalize well. Training in words or phrases improves decoding speed during reading only when the passage is made up of the trained words or phrases (Fleisher et al., 1979). Repeated reading of passages results in faster and more accurate reading of new passages, but only when the new passages are very similar to the trained passages (Dowhower, 1987). Computerized versions of the method (see Carver & Hoffman, 1981, for a description of Programmed Prose) show a similar lack of generalizability of gains to other types of reading tasks.

Repeated reading does not result in improvements in comprehension (Fleisher et al., 1979; Spring, Blunden & Gatherall, 1981). Children trained to automaticity may perceive the task of reading to be fluent word recognition, rather than comprehension of what is read. O'Shea, Sindelar and O'Shea (1985) examined this possibility and found that when comprehension was emphasized to students, both fluency and comprehension increased as the number of repeated readings increased. *Thus, the optimal way to use the method of repeated readings is to have students practice reading passages about four times while cueing them to read for understanding.*

Computer Based Decoding Instruction [T]

Because of the need for lots of practice and controlled feedback, computers are being used as instructional tools to teach decoding skills. "Computers have the capacity to deliver motivating, carefully monitored, individualized and speed oriented practice in concentrations far beyond those available in traditional instructional formats" (Torgeson, 1986, p. 159). The two programs which will be covered here have been well-researched (i.e., Roth and Beck, 1987) and show promise.

Construct-A-Word

In this program, the student is required to compose words from sets of subword letter strings. The student is shown a matrix of sub-word letter strings, and is required to select the appropriate word beginnings and word endings in order to form real words. Figure 2-1 shows an example screen from the program. The task has a game-like quality in that the object of the activity is to construct more words in less time. *Construct-a-Word* provides corrective feedback when the student makes a selection that does not form a real word. The pseudoword is presented aurally and visually, and the student is informed that the string does not spell a word. A student may also request HELP. In response to this command, the computer will aurally present a word that the student has not used. If this hint is not enough to enable the student to construct a word, the program will flash the correct word beginning, and if necessary, the appropriate word ending.

There are 20 levels in the *Construct-a-Word* program, progressing from common CVC combinations found in early reading material to endings using a long vowel/silent e combination to beginning and ending consonant clusters and vowel digraphs in increasingly longer words. The goal of the program was to create a pool of approximately 50 word parts that when

Figure 2-1
Sample screen from Construct-a-Word.

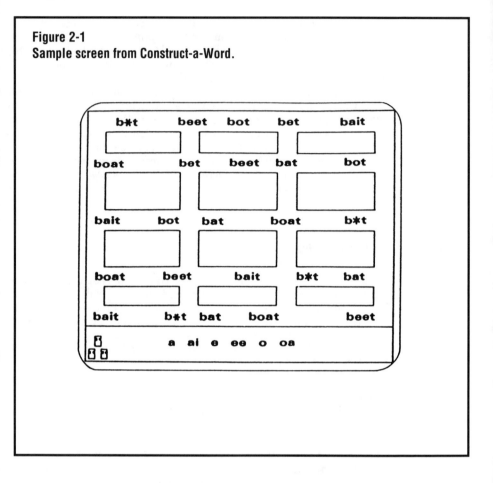

combined across all 20 levels of materials would produce several thousand words. In short, the program was designed to develop generalizable decoding skills.

Hint and Hunt

This program involves attending to subword letter strings during word recognition by encouraging vowel discrimination. The specific goal is to increase the accuracy and efficiency with which vowels and vowel digraphs are used to identify words. A word or pseudoword is presented aurally, and the student must either find or compose a letter string that matches the spoken one. Figure 2-2 illustrates a typical screen of the program.

At each new level of the program, the HINT phase occurs. This is a 5 to

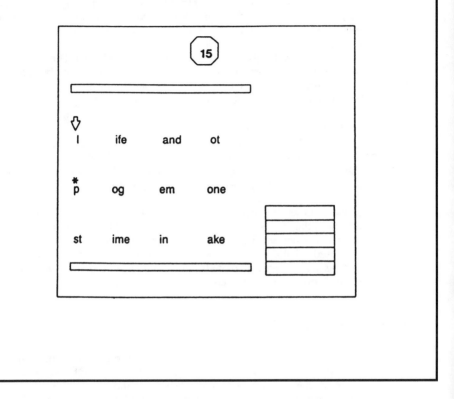

Figure 2-2
Sample screen from Hint and Hunt.

10 minute introduction to the words and vowel discriminations that are covered in that level. The students are aurally and visually presented with examples of strings where the initial and final sounds remain constant while the vowel sound changes. After several examples are presented, the student will see the initial and final letters of the string with the vowels missing. The student will then hear a word, and must fill in the blank with the appropriate vowel or vowel digraph.

The main phase of the program is the HUNT phase. The student is required to match a spoken version of a word or pseudoword to a visual one. This phase has a game-like structure as well, since the student is required to move a ban-shaped cursor through a maze to the nearest letter string that matches the spoken one. Some of the letter strings match the spoken "word" directly, whereas others require the vowel sound to be filled in. Points are accumulated based on the time that elapses before the word is found and selected. The "game" continues until the maze is cleared or the student has lost three "men". Men are lost when an incorrect choice is made or when the time limit is exceeded. The program provides corrective feedback when an incorrect choice is made. The feedback consists of the visual and aural presentation of both the correct and incorrect words. The corrective feedback may be repeated as often as the student desires.

There are 20 levels of materials within *Hint and Hunt*. The first 10 levels focus on the five short vowels and introduce discriminations between these and several digraphs, whereas the later levels focus on vowel digraphs, emphasizing discrimination between the various digraphs.

Evaluation Data

These two methods have been evaluated by Roth and Beck (1987). They found that grade 4 children who received 20-24 hours of instruction with these programs experienced substantial increases in the accuracy and efficiency of decoding and word recognition processes for both laboratory tasks and standardized achievement tests. Decoding improvements were found in tasks that were different from the activities of the instruction. In addition, the effects were not limited to a specific set of words (i.e., those used in instruction). Students' ability to comprehend phrases and sentences increased substantially on laboratory tasks and standardized achievement tests as well. (Experimental students gained more than a year relative to controls on the standardized tests.)

Integrated Picture Training [T]

This mnemonic method involving the use of pictorial memory aids was developed by Ehri, Deffner and Wilce (1984) to teach letter-sound relations to prereaders, usually children in preschool and kindergarten. During the first phase of training, the phonemic segmentation pretraining phase, the children are taught to segment and pronounce the five target sounds they are going to learn. Five common names of people are pronounced, and the children are required to repeat each name and then pronounce the initial sound alone (i.e., Bob, /buh/) to a criterion of 2 flawless trials in a row on 2 sets of names. The children are then given the five object names that serve as mnemonics during letter-sound training, and are taught to segment their initial sounds to a criterion of one perfect trial.

The next phase of training, the letter-sound training phase, involves the training of consonant letters. Objects having names beginning with the response sounds to be associated with the letters are identified (i.e., f, flower). All letters are taught in the lowercase form, except for the letter t, which is taught in the capital form because of its greater resemblance to

Figure 2-3
Sample pictures used during Integrated-Picture Training.

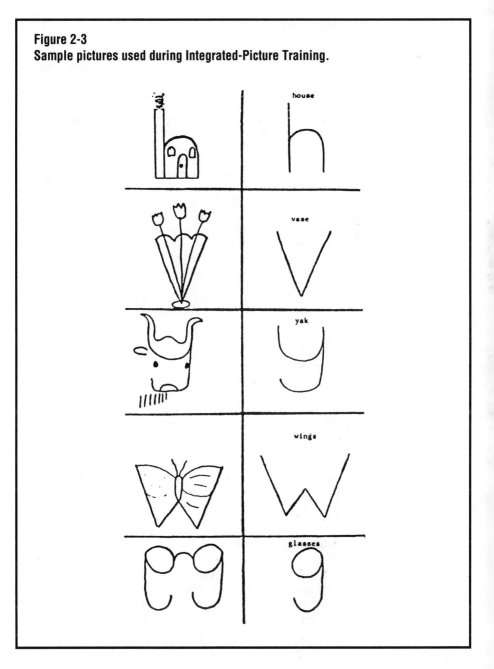

table, its mnemonic picture. Children view integrated pictures, that is, drawings of pictures with the letter responsible for the initial sound embedded in it (i.e., flower with the f as part of the stem). Examples of the types of integrated pictures used during this type of training are shown in Figure 2-3.

Five trials (one per day) are administered. Children are told they will be learning some letters and the sounds that they make, and that they will see pictures that will give them clues about the sounds of the letters. They are also told that the shapes of the pictures will tell them what the letters look like.

The procedure for teaching each letter is as follows. Children are shown a detailed picture of the object. They hear and repeat the object name plus its initial sound. The attention of the children is directed towards the relevant part of the picture. The children are then given a simplified drawing of the object with the appropriate embedded letter, and are told to notice how the picture was drawn to have the shape of the letter. The children are required to name the object, point to the letter, and pronounce its sound. The children are then required to print the letter, and convert their letter into the simplified drawing by adding the relevant details. The final step involves having the children look at the letters again and say the sound it makes. If necessary, the children may be prompted to think of the object name, but they are told not to vocalize the word, just the sound. Corrective feedback is provided during this phase.

A test trial follows each study trial. The children are shown each letter and are told to say the sound it makes. They are encouraged to think of the picture to help remember the sound, but they are to vocalize only the sound and not the word. After each letter has been presented and the child has vocalized the sound, the children are asked to name the picture associated with the letter. If necessary, the children are given the name and are asked to give the initial sound in the name that went with the letter.

Ehri, Deffner and Wilce (1984) found that children receiving integrated-pictures training recalled significantly more letter-sound relations. The authors concluded that integrated-picture mnemonics are helpful for teaching letter-sound relations to prereaders. They also suggested the need to determine if this knowledge can then be used to begin reading words.

Sound Categorization Training [T]

Much research has been conducted examining the relation between rhyming and reading skill (Bradley & Bryant, 1983; Calfee, Chapman & Venezky, 1972). The ability to categorize words on the basis of common sounds, that is, knowledge of rhyme and alliteration, seems to be related to later reading and spelling skill (Bradley & Bryant, 1983, 1985). This connection would seem to be important since both activities involve breaking words and

Table 2-1
Sample sets of words used in Sound Categorization Training.

First Sounds				Middle Sounds					End Sounds			Rhyming Groups		
b	c	h	n	a	e	i	o	u	t	n	g			
bag	cat	hat	net	bag	bed	pig	box	bus	hat	man	bag	bat	hen	band
band	car	hand	nut	cat	hen	fish	cot	cup	nut	hen	leg	mat	men	hand
bat	cot	hen	nest	man	leg	hill	doll	gun	net	gun	dog	cat	pen	land
bed	cup	hair	nail	tap	net	pin	sock	nut	coat	pin	pig	rat	ten	sand
box	coat	hill		mat	peg		fox	sun	rat	sun	peg	hat		
ball	cake	hook		rat	ten		dog		cot	ten				
book	cook													
bus														

syllables into phonological segments. Understanding the relation between the visual or graphemic segments and the sound produced is vital to decoding. Bradley and Bryant (1985) have developed a training program that is based on teaching children to categorize according to sound. The program improves both decoding and spelling skill.

Two principles underlie the technique. The first principle is that the same word can be categorized in the same way in different sets of words. For example, the children are taught that "*hen* starts with the same sound as *hat* and *hand*, and it also starts with the same sound as *hill* and *hair*" (Bradley & Bryant, 1985, p. 80).

The second principle taught is that the same word can be categorized in different ways in successive sets of words. For example, the child is taught that "*hen* starts with the same sound as *hat* and *hand*, ends with the same sound as *men* and *sun*, and has the same middle sound as *bed* and *leg*" (Bradley & Bryant, 1985, p.80). Examples of the types of sets used in sound categorization training by Bradley and Bryant (1985) are reproduced in Table 2-1.

The program involves 40 10-minute sessions. In their early work, these sessions were spread out over 2 years; more recent research has examined the effectiveness of training when the sessions are grouped over 4 months (Bradley, 1988). In the first half of the sessions, 6-year-old children were taught to categorize words on the basis of common sounds using pictures of familiar objects.

The first category of introduced words begins with the letter b̲. A selection of pictures from this group are spread out in front of the child, and the child is asked to name the objects in the pictures. The child is asked to repeat the names, and listen carefully to them. This is repeated, and the child is asked if he/she can hear anything the same about them. The child is encouraged to discover the sound common to the objects in the set. The child is to say what sound it is, in this case, the sound /buh/.

In order to reinforce the concept, the task is repeated with different picture cards. The child is then required to pick out pictures that start with the same sound as *bus*, for example, and is also asked to pick out pictures of things that start with the letter b̲. Next, the child is required to pick out the pictures that do not start with the target letter, or the target sound. The child is asked which pictures go together, and is required to provide reasons for his/her choice. When the child is consistently correct in giving reasons for his/her decision, the next sound category is introduced. This increases the difficulty level of the task, since the child is required to choose between more and more categories (Bradley & Bryant, 1985).

The child also plays *"the odd-one-out-game"* (Bradley & Bryant, 1985). During this task, the child is presented with a number of cards with pictures whose names start with the same letter and one card with a picture whose name starts with another letter. The child is required to pick out the card that does not belong, and to explain his/her choice.

The next stage involves presenting the child with sets of words, and the child has to decide whether the words rhyme or whether they share the same first sound (alliteration). Once the child has mastered this stage, he/she is ready to learn about differences in the end sounds of words. For example, the child is presented with the set *"hat, cat, rat, man"*. *"Man"* is the odd word because it has a different end sound. Task difficulty is increased by introducing the child to words which only share a common final sound, for example, *man* and *pin* (Bradley and Bryant, 1985).

The last sets to be introduced are characterized by words that share a common middle vowel sound. For example, the child is presented with the set *"hat, mat, rat, cot"*, and is asked to pick the odd word. In this example, the child would choose *"cot"*, since it has a different vowel sound from the rest of the words in the set. The task is made more difficult by presenting sets of words which only have common middle vowel sounds, such as *man* and *cat*.

As training progresses, the use of pictures is phased out; thus, the task becomes an aural one. The child is asked to produce words which share a common sound; identify the sound that is common to the words in the set; choose the *"odd one out"* of four spoken words, given the sound in common; choose the *"odd one out"* of four spoken words, not given the common sound; and identify the sound common to three out of four spoken words (Bradley & Bryant, 1985).

During the second half of the training sessions, the use of plastic alphabet letters is introduced. A new sound category is introduced first with the picture cards, as previously described, and then the child is required to make each word in the set with the plastic letters. When the child does not know how to spell the word, the teacher makes the word for him/her. The child is told to look at the word carefully, and then the teacher scrambles the letters. The child is then asked to make the word. This cycle continues until the child spells the word correctly (Bradley, 1988). After successfully spelling the first word, the child is asked to spell the second word in the set. During the first few trials with the plastic letters, the child usually puts away all of the letters before starting on the next word, but as training progresses the child soon learns that many of the letters used for the first word are needed for the rest of the words in the set. In other words, the child learns to keep the sequence common to the words in the set in place and only alter the changing letters.

Evaluation Data

Bradley and her associates have done a commendable job evaluating the efficacy of the sound categorization training program. Children trained in sound categorization were reading at levels 8 months ahead (Schonell Reading Test) and 10 months (Neale Reading Test) ahead of children trained to categorize words conceptually (i.e., rat, bat, cat are all animals). Sound categorization training also resulted in gains in spelling skill: these children were 17 months ahead in Schonell Spelling than children who were taught to categorize words conceptually. The comparisons with control group children, who received no instruction outside of their regular classroom, are even more convincing. Sound categorization trained children were 11 months (Schonell) and 14 months (Neale) ahead in reading, and 23 months ahead in spelling (Schonell).

Bradley has also collected longitudinal data (Bradley, 1987). Four years after sound categorization training, these children were still 10 months ahead of conceptual categorization trained children in reading and 14 months ahead in spelling: gains were maintained. Very few children in the experimental group required remedial reading instruction, whereas many of the control group children required the extra help.

The program has also undergone componential analysis (Bradley & Bryant, 1985; Bradley, 1988). It was found that the largest gains resulted from the use of both phonological (sound categorization) and visual orthographic (plastic letters) strategies. Although the instruction of both strategies separately or either strategy alone resulted in some gains in reading and spelling, the direct instruction of the connection between phonological and orthographic features of language seems to optimize progress in reading and spelling (Bradley, 1988).

Concluding Comment

Considering the importance of good decoding skills, it is alarming that few empirically validated strategies are available for educators to implement in the classroom. Too many researchers seem to be caught up in theoretical issues, and fail to examine the applicability of their models of reading to the classroom.

This state of affairs is even more alarming in light of the fact that poor decoding skills are not just apparent in early readers. Calfee, Lindamood & Lindamood (1973) found that poor readers in kindergarten through grade twelve have failed to master relatively simple word attack skills. Their findings are even more disturbing when one considers that word attack skills are rarely taught after sixth grade. There is a definite need for more study of decoding strategies that can be taught.

Decoding is necessary for good comprehension, however, it is important to note that decoding training does not necessarily result in improved comprehension (Johnson & Baumann, 1984; Just & Carpenter, 1987; Spring, Blunden & Gatherall, 1981). Methods for improving comprehension are taken up in the next chapter.

REFERENCES

Barr, R. (1984). Beginning reading instruction: From debate to reformation. In P. D. Pearson, R. Barr, M. Kamil, & P. Mosenthal (Eds.), *Handbook of reading research* (pp. 545-581). New York: Longman.

Beck, I. L. (1981). Reading problems and instructional practices. In G. E. MacKinnon & T. G. Waller (Eds.), Reading research: *Advances in theory and practice* (vol. 2; pp. 53-95). New York: Academic Press.

Bradley, L. (1987). *Categorizing sounds, early intervention and learning to read: A follow-up study.* Paper presented at the British Psychological Society conference, December, 1987.

Bradley, L. (1988). Making connections in learning to read and to spell. *Applied Cognitive Psychology, 2,* 3-18.

Bradley, L. & Bryant, P. E. (1983). Categorizing sounds and learning to read—a causal connection. *Nature, 301* 419-421.

Bradley, L. & Bryant, P. (1985). *Rhyme and reason in reading and spelling.* International Academy for Research in Learning Disabilities Series. Michigan: University of Michigan Press.

Calfee, R. C., Chapman, R. & Venezky, R. (1972). How a child needs to think to learn to read. In L. W. Gregg (Ed.), *Cognition in learning and memory.* New York: Wiley.

Calfee, R. C., Lindamood, P. & Lindamood, C. (1973).Acoustic-phonetic skills and reading—kindergarten through twelfth grade. *Journal of Educational Psychology, 64,* 293-298.

Carver, R. P. & Hoffman, J. V. (1981). The effect of practice through repeated reading on reading ability using a computer-based instructional system. *Reading Research Quarterly, 16,* 374-390.

Curtis, M. E. (1980). Development of components of reading skill. *Journal of Educational Psychology, 72,* 656-669.

Dowhower, S. L. (1987). Effects of repeated reading on second-grade transitional readers' fluency and comprehension. *Reading Research Quarterly, 22,* 389-406.

Ehri, L. C., Deffner, N. D. & Wilce, L. S. (1984).Pictorial mnemonics for phonics. *Journal of Educational Psychology, 76,* 880-893.

Ehri, L. C. & Wilce, L. S. (1983). Development of word identification speed in skilled and less skilled beginning readers. *Journal of Educational Psychology, 75*, 3-18.

Fleisher, L. S., Jenkins, J. R. & Pany, D. (1979). Effects on poor readers' comprehension of training in rapid decoding. *Reading Research Quarterly, 15*, 30-48.

Frederiksen, J. R. (1981). Sources of process interactions in reading. In A. M Lesgold & C. A. Perfetti (Eds.), *Interactive processes in reading* (pp. 361-386).Hillsdale: Lawrence Erlbaum.

Gettinger, M. (1986). Prereading skills and achievement under three approaches to teaching word recognition. *Journal of Research and Development in Education, 19*, 1-9.

Johnson, D. D. & Baumann, J. F. (1984). Word identification. In P.D. Pearson, R. Barr, M. Kamil & P. Mosenthal (Eds.), *Handbook of reading research* (pp. 583-608). New York: Longman.

Just, M. A. & Carpenter, P. A. (1987). *The psychology of reading and language comprehension.* Newton: Allyn & Bacon.

LaBerge, D. & Samuels, S.J., (1974). Toward a theory of automatic information processing in reading. *Cognitive Psychology, 6*, 293-323.

Lesgold, A. M. & Perfetti, C. A. (1981). Interactive processes in reading: Where do we stand? In A. M. Lesgold and C. A. Perfetti (Eds.), *Interactive processes in reading.* Hillsdale: Lawrence Erlbaum.

O'Shea, L. J, Sindelar, P. T. & O'Shea, D. J, (1985). The effects of repeated readings and attentional cues on reading fluency and comprehension. *Journal of Reading Behavior, 17*, 129-142.

Perfetti, C. A., Finger, E. & Hogaboam, T. (1978). Sources of vocalization latency differences between skilled and less skilled young readers. *Journal of Educational Psychology, 70*, 730-739,

Perfetti, C. A. & Hogaboam, T. (1975). Relationship between single word decoding and reading comprehension skill. *Journal of Educational Psychology, 67*, 461-469.

Perfetti, C. A. & Lesgold, A. M. (1977). Discourse comprehension and sources of individual differences. In M. A. Just & P. A. Carpenter (Eds.), *Cognitive processes in comprehension.* Hillsdale: Lawrence Erlbaum.

Perfetti, C. A. & Roth, S. (1981). Some of the interactive processes in reading and their role in reading skill. In A. M. Lesgold & C. A. Perfetti (Eds.), *Interactive processes in reading* (pp. 269-297). Hillsdale: Lawrence Erlbaum.

Pflaum, S. W., Walberg, H. J., Karegianes, M. L. & Rasher, S. P. (1980). Reading instruction: a quantitative analysis. *Educational Researcher, 9*, 12-18.

Roth, S. F. & Beck, I. L. (1987). Theoretical and Instructional implications of the assessment of two microcomputer word recognition programs. *Reading Research Quarterly, 22*, 197-218.

Samuels, S. J, (1979). The method of repeated readings. *The Reading Teacher, 32*, 403-408.

Spring, C., Blunden, D. & Gatherall, M. (1981). Effect on reading comprehension of training to automaticity in word-reading. *Perceptual and Motor Skills, 53*, 779-786.

Taylor, I. & Taylor, M. M. (1983). *The psychology of reading.* New York: Academic Press.

Torgeson, J. K. (1986). Computers and cognition in reading: A focus on decoding fluency. *Exceptional Children, 53*, 157-162.

Underwood, G. (1985). Information processing in skilled readers. In G. E. MacKinnon & T. G. Waller (Eds.), *Reading research: Advances in theory and practice* (vol. 4, pp. 139-181). Orlando: Academic Press.

Vellutino, F. R. & Scanlon, D. M. (1986). Experimental evidence for the effects of instructional bias on word identification. *Exceptional Children, 53*, 145-155.

CHAPTER 3

Reading Comprehension Strategies

In this chapter, we describe reading strategies that can be taught to elementary-grade children, with an emphasis on ones that can be taught in less than 10 hours of class time. All of these are strategies that children in grades 3 through 8 could learn to execute by themselves. Many of these strategies are approaches that are used spontaneously by competent readers.

Our discussion of each strategy begins with a brief rationale to orient the teacher to the strategy. How to teach the strategy is then presented with various approaches to instructing the strategy. The scientific evidence supporting the effectiveness of each strategy is reviewed as are gaps in the research that may leave questions as to the strategy's general utility.

Summarization [SSR]

A single reading rarely permits recall of all information in a text. Mature readers usually abstract the gist, or macrostructure, of what they read (Kintsch & van Dijk, 1978). This macrostructure resembles a summary of the passage in that trivial details are not included and generalizations are made that sum up the passage. Summarization, or abstraction of the macrostructure, is thought to be an integral part of competent reading (Kintsch & van Dijk, 1978). Children, however, have difficulty producing summaries of text passages unless they are taught how to do so (Brown & Day, 1983; Brown, Day, & Jones, 1983). Thus, a number of investigators have provided summarization instruction to children.

There have been many approaches to instructing summarization. The simplest involves producing single sentences that capture the meaning of entire paragraphs (Doctorow, Wittrock, & Marks, 1978; Jenkins, Heliotis, Stein, & Haynes, 1987). The simplicity of this approach is appealing, but retention of isolated facts has been the only measure used to evaluate it. Although this basic form of summarization has been effective in improving memory of isolated facts, the general utility of this approach has not been established since it has not been evaluated using more general comprehension or memory measures.

A more complex and theoretically well-grounded approach includes instruction of the rules that Kintsch and van Dijk (1978) identified as the basis for summaries constructed by mature readers. These rules include (e.g., Brown & Day, 1983):

(1) Delete trivial information.
(2) Delete redundant information.
(3) Substitute superordinate terms for lists of items.
(4) Integrate a series of events with a superordinate action term.
(5) Select a topic sentence.
(6) Invent a topic sentence if there is none.

Bean and Steenwyk (1984) successfully taught grade-6 children to apply these rules to single paragraphs. Summarization instruction improved the children's recall of paragraphs. More impressive, however, was the finding that the children trained to use the summarization rules did better on a standardized reading comprehension test than did children who were not instructed to summarize paragraphs.

Summarization instruction has also been extended to prose that is longer than single paragraphs. Children have been taught to construct summaries of passages that are as long as those commonly contained in middle-grade science and social studies texts (i.e., 800- to 2500-word passages). For example, Taylor and Beach (1984) taught seventh-grade children to summarize 6-10 page (approximately 2500-word) social studies passages. During 7 one-hour sessions, the children were taught how to produce and study a hierarchical summary of a reading passage. A hierarchical summary consists of a thesis statement at the top of the page that is followed by main idea statements; each main idea statement has two or three supporting ideas for each section of the text, and topic headings are written in the margins to connect the sections (see Table 3-1 for an example of a hierarchical summary). Taylor and Beach taught the students to outline each sub-section before constructing the thesis statement for the entire passage. The teacher helped students generate the summaries for the first four sessions, and the students produced summaries independently for the remaining three sessions. During each session, the class discussed their summaries with the teacher and compared their summaries to the prototypical summaries provided by Taylor and Beach (1984). After producing the summaries, the students were instructed to study them for five minutes to try to remember as much of the content as possible. This summarization training proved successful in that recall of subsequent passages was improved compared to that of students not trained in summary production.

Rinehart, Stahl, and Erickson (1986) used a similar method to train grade-school children to produce summaries that include main ideas with supporting information so that the summary reflected the organization of the original text. The instruction was based on two of Kintsch and van Dijk's (1978) rules - delete trivial information and delete redundant information-

Table 3-1
Hierarchical Summary for a Three-Page Social Studies Passage

1. Johnson developed programs to fight injustice and poverty.

Civil Rights
    A. *Lyndon Johnson became President of the U.S. after Kennedy was assassinated.* hard worker, tried to carry out some of Kennedy's programs.
    B. *Johnson fought for civil-rights law.* to protect blacks from discrimination in hotels and restaurants, blacks had not been allowed in some hotels or restaurants in the South.
    C. *Johnson persuaded Congress to pass a law ensuring all people the right to vote.* protected black people's right to vote, literacy tests now illegal.
    D. *Johnson started a "war on poverty".* job training, education for poor people, plans for a "Great Society".

Great Society Programs
    E. *Johnson persuaded Congress to develop medicare* for people at least 65 years old, hospital bills paid, doctor's bills paid in part.
    F. *Johnson persuaded Congress to pass a law giving money to schools.* to improve education for poor families, one billion dollars in aid to schools.

Adapted from Taylor and Beach (1984).

and another summarization technique, relate main to supporting information (Taylor & Beach, 1982). Rinehart et al.'s (1986) instruction was provided over the course of five 45-50 minute sessions.

First, the teacher defined a summary as *"the important information from a reading"* (p.429) and explained its utility in reading and studying. The teacher modeled how to write down only main ideas and supporting information by *"talking through"* four sample paragraphs and having individual children do similar *"talk-throughs"*. Next, the teacher modeled use of the following checklist to be used by students during the first three lessons:

(1) Have I found the overall idea that the paragraph or group of paragraphs is about?
(2) Have I found the most important information that tells more about the overall idea?
(3) Have I used any information that is not directly about the overall idea?
(4) Have I used any information more than once?

During the second lesson, students practiced summarizing single para-graphs while the teacher provided individual and class feedback. The third lesson consisted of summarizing groups of paragraphs. The students were taught to summarize individual paragraphs first and then to summarize the summaries. Again, teacher modeling and discussion was followed by teacher-monitored student practice. The fourth step involved summarizing passages of several paragraphs without first summarizing individual para-graphs. The students were instructed to write the overall idea for the passage, and then to add the most important supporting ideas from the passage in as few sentences as possible. The final lesson included practice of the passage length version of the summarization strategy. Students prac-ticed writing summaries of each section of a textbook chapter. Table 3-2 provides an outline of the principles and procedures used by Rinehart et al. (1986). Use of this strategy by the trained students improved their recall of main ideas from passages compared to students not trained to use the summarization strategy.

Table 3-2
Summarization Instruction

A. Teach four rules for producing summaries:
   (1) Identify main information.
   (2) Delete trivial information.
   (3) Delete redundant information.
   (4) Relate main and supporting information.

B. Base teaching on principles of direct instruction and self-control training:
   (1) Use explicit explanation - teach why, when, and where to apply the skill.
   (2) Model skills - talk through examples, showing how the skill is applied.
   (3) Provide practice with feedback.
   (4) Break complex skills down - summarize short paragraphs before proceeding to longer passages.
   (5) Use scripted lessons to provide guidance to your instruction.
   (6) Program self-control - phase out teacher direction and phase in student control throughout instruction.

C. Three steps to follow in summarizing multiple-paragraph essays:
   (1) Write summaries of each paragraph.
   (2) Create a summary of the paragraph summaries.
   (3) Apply the four summarization rules to this paragraph.

From Rinehart, Stahl, and Erickson (1986)

Summarization training can also include spatial components. Baumann (1984) included graphic metaphors as part of his summarization instruction with sixth-grade students. For example, students were taught to think of the main idea as a table top supported by details as represented by the legs of the table. This training improved children's summary writing, but not their recall of text. However, Baumann (1984) did not emphasize the Kintsch and van Dijk (1978) rules of summarization or the utility of graphic metaphors. Berkowitz (1986), on the other hand, emphasized use of summarization rules and spatial outlining in her research. Grade-6 students were taught to construct maps of passages over the course of six 45-minute sessions. Students were taught to write the title of the passage in the center of a sheet of paper. They then surveyed the text for four to six main ideas. These ideas were placed in a circle around the title. Then, students wrote two to four important supporting details under each main idea. Students were taught to use the graphic summary as a test until they could recite the main ideas and the supporting details. Overall recall of passages was improved by use of this graphic summarizing strategy.

Armbruster, Anderson, and Ostertag (1987) taught fifth-grade children about the problem/solution structure that characterizes many social studies passages. This structure includes statement of a problem, actions taken to solve the problem, and the results of the actions. Students learned to use this structure to organize summaries of problem/solution passages into three-box diagrams depicting problem, actions, and results. The instruction proceeded over eleven 45-minute sessions in which the children were told that summarizing in this way would facilitate learning of text. The children were given a lot of practice summarizing social studies passages using the problem/solution framework. The training resulted in improved recall of text. Again, summarization instruction improved memory for what was read.

We recommend instructing students to produce summaries while they read. Summarization instruction improves children's recall of what they read compared to children who are taught using traditional reading comprehension instruction (Armbruster et al., 1987; Berkowitz, 1986; Taylor & Beach, 1984). Summarization training is a powerful intervention because many variations of the technique have proven successful.

There are several cautionary notes that should be added to this generally positive evaluation. First, research has not been conducted on summarization with normal children younger than 10 years of age. The only data on children younger than 10 were produced by Jenkins et al. (1987) who trained grade-3 and grade-4 learning disabled children to write brief restatements of single paragraphs. Second, teachers need to monitor students' progress in acquiring the strategy. In her investigations with grade-5 students, Taylor (1982) found that when students had not mastered the strategy, there was little evidence of improved performance. Third, there has been little study of how much training time is required to teach summarization. Most studies provided at least six hours of instruction, suggesting that students require ample opportunity for practice to master the strategy. Finally, successful summarization interventions seem to require active student involvement in generating summaries. For instance, Berkowitz (1986) observed only small effects when prepared summaries were provided to elementary-school students. There are clear benefits, however, when students master the strategy of summarization and generate summaries themselves.

Mental Imagery [SSR]

Construction of mental images while reading is another strategy that has been demonstrated to improve children's memory for prose (Pressley, 1977). The use of imagery in reading has a sound theoretical base in dual-coding theory (Paivio, 1971). According to this theory, imagery should aid reading comprehension because both a verbal memory code and an imaginal memory code are activated. Dual coding of prose should aid later recall in that the two codes could be expected to leave a stronger memory trace than a verbal code alone, making it easier to recall the information later.

Two different approaches to construction of images have been investigated. The first is representational imagery in which the images represent precisely the content of the prose. Consider the sentence, *"The kitten clung to the clothesline while the dog glared at it from below"*. A representational image for that sentence would include a kitten hanging by its paws with a dog on the ground below. It is possible to construct a representational image of this sentence because the elements (kitten, clothesline, dog) are all easily imaginable. Most readers possess concrete images for these objects. Sometimes, however, prose contains elements that are not as easily imagined. Consider the sentence, *"Mr. McGoldrick planted potatoes in a large field"*. While most people could construct an image of a man planting potatoes in a large field, few people would have a concrete image of someone named Mr. McGoldrick. In this case, a proxy, or keyword mnemonic, for McGoldrick could be generated - that is, a word that can be linked to the concept for which an image cannot be generated. Readers might notice that the name McGoldrick contains the word "gold". Imagining a man who is planting potatoes suddenly unearthing gold would make the sentence memorable. When asked later, What did *Mr. McGoldrick do?"*, the name McGoldrick could cue the mnemonic element "gold", which would lead back to the image of a man planting potatoes in a large field.

Representational Imagery

Representational imagery facilitates children's learning of text after the age of eight, at least when children are reading concrete stories. Representational imagery has a positive effect on short-answer recall tests (Pressley, 1977; Pierce, 1980). Sadoski (1983, 1985) also demonstrated that children in grades 3, 4, and 5 who report spontaneous use of representational imagery have a better understanding of complex relationships in prose than do children who do not report imagery use. Although the effects produced by representational imagery are relatively small, the evidence is consistent and, hence, we recommend teaching this strategy to elementary-school children. Our enthusiasm for this strategy is also fueled by the fact that children can be taught to use representational imagery quickly and easily.

Pressley (1976) taught third-grade children to construct representational images for prose material in approximately 20 minutes. Training began by having children practice forming images with sentences. The children were taught by the researcher in groups of four to six. After forming an image of a sentence like "The man sat in his chair and smoked his pipe", the children were shown a picture representing the contents of the sentence to demonstrate what their images might look like. It was stressed that the children's images did not have to look exactly like the instructor's pictures. The training proceeded from practice with sentences to practice with paragraphs and a short story. The children were instructed not to try to read and construct images at the same time since both involve the visual system and could interfere with each other. The children were taught to read a section of the text and then to stop reading and to imagine what was conveyed in the text. Children who were taught this strategy could recall more of a 950-word story - one not accompanied by any pictures - than could children who were not taught the strategy.

Gambrell and Bales (1986) provided evidence that representational imagery has a larger effect when measures other than short-answer recall are obtained. They used detection of text inconsistencies as their outcome measure (e.g., Markman, 1981). Gambrell and Bales (1986) taught poor readers from the 4th and 5th grades to construct images representing prose, with instruction proceeding from sentence-length to paragraph-length material. The entire training took 30 minutes and consisted of telling children, "One good way to understand and remember what you read is to make pictures in your mind. I want you to make pictures in your mind to help you understand and remember what you read" (p.458).

To test whether representational imagery aided detection of text inconsistencies, children read two passages containing inconsistencies after being told that someone was attempting to write short stories for children. They were asked to read the stories to see if they made sense and were prompted to "make pictures in your mind to determine if there is anything that is not clear and easy to understand about the story" (p.459). One of the passages contained the following sentences, "The blindfolded pigeons could not use their eyes. All of the pigeons were able to find their way home. They were able to use the sun to find their way home" (p.437). After reading a passage, the student was probed to determine if the inconsistencies had been detected. The questioning began without any hint that there might be a problem. Thus, the child was asked, 'What do you think about the passage about pigeons? Do you have any suggestions? Did the author forget to put in any information?" (p.458). If the child did not detect the inconsistency with these questions, they were asked questions that contained hints (e.g., "Was there anything that was not clear and that was not easy to understand? Could blindfolded pigeons use their eyes?")

The main finding in this study was that children trained to use representational imagery detected more inconsistencies than did children who were not trained to use imagery. The untrained children were given all of the same prose and asked to do whatever would help them remember it. Again, representational imagery was demonstrated to improve reading comprehension with minimal investment of instructional time and effort. Children's reading comprehension was improved by having them construct images that represented the content of the written material. It should be emphasized that the instruction outlined here began with sentence-length material before proceeding to longer passages.

Mnemonic Imagery [T & SSR]

Research on mnemonic imagery as a reading comprehension strategy has largely been restricted to the study of an intervention known as the *keyword method* (McCormick & Levin, 1984; Shriberg, Levin, McCormick, & Pressley, 1982). For instance, Levin, Shriberg, and Berry (1983) read passages to eighth-grade students describing the attributes of fictitious towns (e. g., the town of "Fostoria" was noted for its abundant natural resources, advances in technology, considerable wealth, and growing population). Students were first taught a *keyword* for the town name, that is, *a well-known word that sounded like part of the town name* (e. g., "frost" for Fostoria). Then, the students were provided with a picture in which frost covered all of the town attributes (i.e., oil pumps representing natural resources, computers for advanced technology, money for wealth, and many people with young children for the growing population). Figure 3-1 is a black-and-white line-drawn version of the colored picture shown to students as an example of what their image might look like. In other words, during instruction the students were provided with an interactive picture of the keyword (representing the town) and all of the to-be-remembered attributes. Compared to students who were not given keyword mnemonic pictures, these students recalled more of the attributes when later presented with the town names.

In Levin et al. (1983), the descriptions of the towns were read to the students. Peters and Levin (1986) extended the mnemonic representational approach by having the students read 200-word descriptions of famous people. They conducted two experiments in which grade-8 students learned about famous people using the keyword method. In the first experiment, the famous people were fictitious with names that were easily convertible to keywords (e.g., Charlene Fidler and Larry Taylor). The children successfully learned to generate keywords as well as mnemonic images in which the keyword referent interacted with the accomplishments of the famous people. Training in the keyword method improved recall of the accomplishments of the "famous" people.

Figure 3-1
Keyword mnemonic picture
for learning the characteristics
of the town "Fostoria"

Reprinted from Levin, Shriberg, & Berry (1983) by permission of the authors and the American Educational Research Association.

The second experiment conducted by Peters and Levin (1986) involved teaching eighth-grade students to use the keyword method to learn the accomplishments of actual famous people. Generating keywords required some transformation of the names since the names were not created to be easily convertible to keywords (e.g., the keywords for James Smithson were jam and smile, respectively). The experimenters provided the students with the keywords in this experiment (i.e., the students were not expected to generate their own keywords). The students practiced using the keyword method with two passages before being tested on eight other 200-word passages. The instructor provided pictures to which students could compare their images during practice. The students spent only 2 minutes 45 seconds on each passage, including reading and generating keyword mnemonics. Despite the small amount of time, the effects produced by the keyword method were large. The small amount of instructional time expended was well-rewarded in terms of student recall.

Mnemonic imagery is useful when trying to learn information about totally unfamiliar concepts, such as the accomplishments of unfamiliar people or information about unknown countries. It seems especially useful when there are a great many previously unknown concepts that must be learned in a short time.

More work is required to determine precisely the types of text for which mnemonic imagery is appropriate, the utility of the method for younger children, and whether children can be taught to generate their own keywords. However, we are optimistic that the keyword method will prove to be a potent strategy that can be taught quickly and efficiently. As a final note, recent evidence suggests that students seem struck by the effectiveness of mnemonic imagery when they use it, with their enthusiasm related to future use of the strategy (Beuhring & Kee, 1987). Enthusiasm for use of a strategy increases the probability of long-term benefits of instruction.

Question Generation [SSR]

Students can be asked to generate think-type questions, ones that integrate the material covered in a text. The strategy is hypothesized to work either by making readers more active while reading (Singer & Donlan, 1982) or by increasing student awareness of whether they are comprehending (Davey & McBride, 1986). Generating good think-type questions may highlight problems in comprehension and prompt the reader to engage in actions to compensate for comprehension failure.

The instructional effectiveness of this strategy with children is difficult to assess because most question-generation research has been conducted with high school or college students. When the approach has been used with children, it has been as one of several strategies in an effective instructional package (e.g., Palincsar & Brown, 1984), making it difficult to discern the worth of question generation alone. The data with children that can be interpreted suggest modest effects: Wong (1985) reported that the gains produced by question generation are modest when they are obtained at all. More recently, Denner and Rickards (1987) and McDonald (1986) found that very brief instruction in question generation does not improve memory of what is read.

Thus far, our assessment of the effects of question generation has been fairly negative. However, a recent, well controlled study with grade-school children (Davey & McBride, 1986) permits optimism about question generation as a strategy to improve comprehension and memory for what is read. Most other research on question generation with children has only asked children to generate questions or included very brief instruction about how to generate questions. Davey and McBride (1986), on the other hand, showed that reading comprehension and memory for prose are improved if grade-school children are actually taught *how* to generate questions as they read.

Davey and McBride (1986) trained grade-6 children to generate questions over five 40-minute sessions. The instruction provided in this study was successful. First, children who received the full instructional procedure learned to generate better think-type questions than any of the groups to which they were compared. Second, there were moderate to large differences favoring the question-trained group for memory of inferential information. The effect was not as dramatic for memory of literal information but this is not surprising given the focus on inferential information during question-generation training.

The training approach used by Davey and McBride (1986) is summarized in Table 3-3. During the first lesson, students were given a general overview of the activities they would be engaged in during instruction, and an explanation of the value of using question generation while reading. According to our perspective, this is an important step in any strategy instruction. If learners are expected to use strategies, they must understand that the strategies will help. Students were also taught the difference between locate (literal) and think-type (inferential) questions during this first session.

The second lesson consisted of a review of the distinction between think and locate questions and the rationale for generating good think-type questions after reading was further developed. For example, students were told that asking themselves questions would help them know if they need to re-read, help them to remember, and help them predict test questions. Students were also taught how to generate question stems to relate information from one part of a passage to information from another part of the passage. The teacher discussed important words for question stems and good responses to their own questions.

During the third lesson, the teacher reviewed what was taught in previous sessions, and students practiced generating questions related to the most important ideas of a passage. The teacher demonstrated how to decide what is most important in a passage and how to generate questions

Table 3
Principles of Davey and McBride's (1986)
Question-Generation Instructional Procedure

Explain the Rationale and Basics
Explain why generating 'think-type' questions will help comprehension. Explain and practice identifying the distinction between think and locate questions.

Teach How to Generate Questions
Have students practice generating questions while you provide feedback regarding whether they are good 'think-type' questions.

Teach How to Identify Important Information
Demonstrate and have students practice identifying the most important information in passages. Have students practice generating questions related to this content.

Teach Students How to Monitor their own Strategy Use
Provide children with questions to be used to monitor their own use of the question generation strategy, e.g. "How well did I identify important information?"

Provide Practice and Feedback
Provide ample opportunity to practice generating questions, identifying important information, and monitoring strategy use. Provide feedback on each of these aspects during instruction.

related to this content.

Children were taught to evaluate their use of the question generation strategy in the fourth lesson. They were given five monitoring questions to answer as they generated their own questions:
"How well did I identify important information?",
"How well did I link information together?",
"How well could I answer my question?",
"Did my 'think' question use different language from the text?", and
"Did I use good signal words?" (p.258).
Signal words are question words that require integration from one part of the text to another (e.g., What did the author describe previously. . . ?)

The final training session provided students with additional opportunity to practice generating questions. Throughout instruction, students were given the opportunity to practice generating questions, answering questions, and responding to the self-evaluation questions designed to promote student monitoring of their strategy use. Practice was always integrated with teacher feedback regarding student progress and success using the strategy.

In recommending question-generation training, we emphasize the comprehensive nature of Davey and McBride' s (1986) training procedure. Davey and McBride tested the components of their model and found that the full instructional package was more effective than less comprehensive approaches at improving the quality of questions generated and increasing the amount of information recalled from reading passages. Thus, in recommending teaching this strategy to grade-school children, we suggest that the strategy be taught using Davey and McBride's (1986) complete format. Question-generation training should include an explanation of why it is good to self-question while reading, practice using the strategy, feedback regarding students' use of the strategy, and information about how to monitor the use of the strategy. Question generation is probably appropriate for use with both expository and narrative text. Davey and McBride (1986) used expository text, but there is no obvious reason why the strategy would not have the same potential benefits with narrative text. Finally, we re-emphasize the need for research on the effects of question-generation training with child populations other than average sixth-grade readers.

Question-Answering Strategies [SSR]

Teachers and textbooks frequently provide children with questions based on text, with the expectation that answering questions will improve learning. Questions are usually provided after children have read a narrative or a textbook chapter. Questions are thought to help by leading to reprocessing of text, especially when the answers to the questions are not known. Such post-questions have been effective in improving learning by adults (Anderson & Biddle, 1975), but the effects of post-questions with children are much less consistent (e.g., Levin & Pressley, 1981; Pressley & Forrest-Pressley, 1985; Rowls, 1976). However, recent evidence suggests a reason for the inconsistent findings -children may not reprocess text when they do not know the answers to questions. That is, many children do not look back to the text when they have difficulty answering questions (Garner, Hare, Alexander, Haynes, & Winograd, 1984). This is especially true of young children and poor readers in the upper elementary grades. Hence, it has been suggested that children need to be taught strategies to improve their use of questions.

Lookbacks
One such strategy is the "lookback" strategy which involves looking back to the text only for questions that might be answered in the text, focusing on parts of the text that might contain the answer, and integrating across

sentences and phrases to produce an answer. Garner, McCready, and Wagoner (1984) reported that a minority of their grade-5 subjects used such a mature lookback strategy.

Garner, et al. (1984) have conducted initial work to determine if children who do not use the text lookback strategy can be trained to do so. They taught 12 children between 9 and 13 years of age who were experiencing reading difficulties to look back when they could not answer postquestions. The children were taught the lookback strategy in three 20-minute sessions over a period of three days. During the first session, children read two 200-word expository passages and answered three questions. They were told *why* looking back at the text to find the answers should help (*"You cannot remember everything you read"*). During the second session, the *why* hint was reviewed and another expository passage with three questions was read. Children were then told *when* looking back at the text should help (*"for questions that ask about what specific articles or authors said, not about what you think"*). On the third day, children were given another passage with three questions and the lookback strategy was modeled by the teacher to show the children *where* to look for the answers (*"skim the whole article to find the part that might have the answer"*). The instruction of this strategy is summarized in Table 3-4.

Table 3-4
Question-Answering Strategies

A. Text Lookback
Successful readers know these three things about looking back to text to answer questions:
1. *Why look back?*
   You cannot remember everything you read.
2. *When should you look back?*
   When questions ask about what articles or authors said, not about what you think.
3. *Where should you look?*
   Skim the whole article to find the part that might have the right answer.

B. Question-Answer Relationships (Raphael and colleagues)
1. *Right There* - words used to create the question and words used for the answer are "right there" in the same sentence
2. *Think and Search* - the answer is in the text, but words used to create the question and those used for an appropriate answer would be found in two or more sentences
3. *On My Own* - the answer is not found in the text, rather you would think to yourself that you have to find the answer "on your own"

The results of Garner et al.'s (1984) training are clear. Students trained to use lookbacks were more likely than control subjects to use lookbacks when they did not know the answer to a question that was located in the text. The probability of correct answers to the post-questions was higher in the lookback trained condition, with the advantage due to lookback subjects being more likely to find correct answers when they did look back.

As optimistic as these results may seem, we emphasize that this strategy is recommended provisionally, given that more detailed investigation of this strategy is warranted. First, Garner et al. (1984) did not include measures of memory or comprehension for text after children had answered questions on the passage. Second, the questions were worded such that it was obvious when the passage would provide the answer to the question (i.e., questions contained phrases like, "in the article" and "what did the author write"). Real-world questions are often less explicit about where to find the answers.

Question-Answer Relationships [SSR]

Where to find answers to questions is the focus of another question-answering strategy investigated by Raphael and her colleagues (Raphael & McKinney, 1983; Raphael & Pearson, 1985; Raphael & Wonnacott, 1985). Because some children do not know where to find answers to questions, these researchers have taught elementary students question-answer relationships (QARs). The children in these studies were taught to analyze questions to decide if they could be answered by information stated in the text ("right there" questions) by information that could be inferred by combining pieces of information in text ("think and search" questions), or by information in the reader's knowledge base ("on my own" questions).

There was clear evidence that instruction about the relationships between questions and answers increased correct responding to questions following a reading selection. In general, the results were more striking with younger children (fourth graders) than with older students (eighth graders) and with average- and lower-ability children than with high-ability children. It should also be pointed out that the effects produced by this strategy are not very large. As with the lookback strategy, it is also not possible to make the case that improved responding to the questions improved comprehension or long-term memory of the passage, since there has been no clear test of this possibility to date.

Raphael and colleagues have used both teachers and researchers to instruct QARs. In general, QAR instruction was conducted in groups within classrooms as follows. Students received four days of instruction, each session lasting approximately 40 minutes. On the first day, students were introduced to the concept of QAR, being given definitions and visual presentations of the three types of QARs. For example, a picture of a child thinking with an open book might accompany the teacher's explanation of "think and search" questions. Following the introduction, students were given brief passages (2-3 sentences) with three questions (one of each QAR type). The three types of QARs are described in Table 3-4. At first, students were provided with answers to the questions as well as justifications for why the question fit the QAR category. Over the next three sessions, the passages became longer (400 words) with more questions and the students were expected to answer the questions, identify QAR classification, and justify QAR choice themselves. Teachers provided feedback on accuracy of answers, QAR category, and justification for QAR choice.

To summarize the data on the question-answering strategies, we emphasize that children's question answering can be improved by training in how to answer comprehension questions that accompany text. Children can be taught to look back to text to find answers to questions and they can be taught to discriminate opinion questions from those for which answers would be stated explicitly in text. Although we might expect improved question answering to increase long-term learning from text, we cannot make this conclusion based on the research to this point. Therefore, we emphasize our provisional recommendation of the question-answering strategies.

Story Grammar [SSR]

Conventional stories share a general structure (Stein & Glenn, 1979). They begin with a setting that may include information about the time of the story, where it took place, and the central characters. An initiating event then sets a goal or problem. This is followed by an internal response by the characters which, in turn, is followed by actions, or attempts to achieve the goal or solve the problem. Finally, there are consequences of the characters' actions and the characters' reactions to the resolutions. Skilled, mature readers definitely know this story grammar and use it automatically to facilitate comprehension and memory of stories (Mandler, 1984). There is evidence to suggest that poor elementary-school readers possess less well-developed knowledge of story grammar than do their good-reader peers (Rahman & Bisanz, 1986). This leads to the hypothesis that poor readers would benefit from training in story-grammar elements.

The strongest support for this hypothesis comes from a study reported by Short and Ryan (1984). They trained grade-4 boys to use story grammar while reading stories. Following training, the text recall of poor readers was comparable to that of skilled fourth-grade readers. Short and Ryan (1984) trained the children to ask themselves (and answer) the following five questions as they read stories:
(1) Who is the main character?
(2) Where and when did the story take place?
(3) What did the main character do?
(4) How did the story end?
(5) How did the main character feel?

Instruction proceeded through three 30-35 minute individual instructional sessions conducted by the experimenter. The first session included modeling of the story grammar strategy by the experimenter through a taped example. Story grammar was introduced as a game called *Clue*, with a Story-Teller who provided clues that enabled predictions about what would happen in the story and a Detective Reader who searched for the clues in the story to answer the five story-grammar questions. During the second and third training sessions, the story-grammar strategy was reviewed and children practiced using it with three stories. Children were prompted to use the strategy while reading and to underline and label the answers to the questions.

Story grammar has also been taught using story maps (Idol, 1987; Idol & Croll, 1987). Nine- to twelve-year-old children were taught to construct maps that recorded the setting, problem, goal, action, and outcome information (see Figure 3-2). The story-map training was administered by teachers in classrooms containing 22 children. The teacher modeled use of the strategy and children practiced constructing maps. Story-map training is an extension of the Short and Ryan (1984) training to classroom instruction, with essentially the same questions being asked in both types of training. Idol's story-map training improved poor readers' memory for a story. However, the story-grammar training was not necessary for normal readers, a finding that is consistent with the hypothesis that good readers already possess story-grammar knowledge (see also Dreher & Singer, 1980).

The studies reviewed thus far indicate that story-grammar training is effective only for below-average readers. However, Nolte and Singer (1985) reported that a slight variation on story-grammar training improved recall of story facts by normal fourth- and fifth-grade readers. Children were taught to ask themselves questions about the setting, the main characters, the goals of the characters, and the obstacles encountered on the way to the goal. This training differs from other story-grammar training in that the students generated their own questions. Short and Ryan (1984) and Idol's group (Idol, 1987; Idol & Croll, 1987) provided questions to the students. Nolte & Singer (1985) combined question-generation and story-grammar training. Teaching of this strategy occurred over ten 40-minute sessions. As in most strategy instruction, instruction began with teacher explanations and modeling. Guidance was faded until all students were using the strategy autonomously.

To summarize, we recommend story-grammar training, especially for poor readers who may not have sufficient knowledge about narrative structure. Teaching poor readers to identify story-grammar elements helps students remember what they read.

When teaching story grammar, the teacher should model and explain the approach followed by student practice. Teacher prompting and feedback is gradually faded as the students' proficiency in strategy execution increases. The story-grammar strategy appears to be relatively easy to teach in that there are gains after only a few sessions of instruction with poor

Figure 3-2
Components of the Story Map

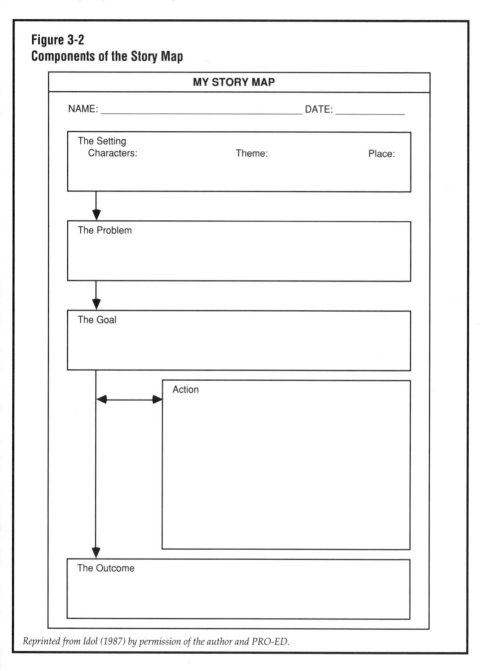

Reprinted from Idol (1987) by permission of the author and PRO-ED.

readers. The story grammar strategy is also easily adaptable to classroom situations using story maps (Idol, 1987; Idol & Croll, 1987). Finally, for good readers the strategy may prove useful if students are taught to generate their own inferential questions aimed at story-grammar elements. Good readers may benefit from generating their own higher-level questions related to story structure.

Activating Prior Knowledge [SSR]

The reader's knowledge base, or prior knowledge of a topic, plays an important role in reading comprehension (Wilson & Anderson, 1986). The way in which text is interpreted or remembered depends on the prior knowledge the reader brings to the reading (e.g., Anderson, Reynolds, Schallert, & Goetz, 1977; Bransford & Johnson, 1973; Pearson, Hansen, & Gordon, 1979). The general finding is that readers who have a well-developed knowledge base recall more relevant information than do readers with less knowledge of the topic covered in the text (Chiesi, Spilich, & Voss, 1979). Activating prior knowledge of a topic while reading would appear to be a good strategy to improve reading comprehension. However, children often do not activate their prior knowledge spontaneously while reading even when they possess knowledge relevant to the topic (Paris & Lindauer, 1976).

Hansen and Pearson (1983) designed an instructional program to teach fourth-grade children to activate prior knowledge in hopes of improving inferential comprehension. The instruction consisted of pre-and post-reading group discussions. Hansen and Pearson (1983) rationalized that group discussion would be the best way to utilize prior knowledge because it is likely to increase the knowledge base of all children. For instance, children with less knowledge of a topic would benefit from the better-developed knowledge bases of their peers.

Hansen and Pearson (1983) provided instruction over the course of 10 weeks, with two sessions per week. The prereading discussion began with a rationale for why it was beneficial to discuss previous experiences that are similar to situations presented in text to be read. The teacher oriented the students with statements such as, "Today, pretend you are reading a science article about conservation. What might you be thinking about while you are reading the article?" (p.823). Following the general discussion, the teacher provided three important ideas from each reading passage and asked students to relate previous experiences to the main ideas and to make predictions about the contents of the stories, based on the ideas. After reading the passages, the class discussed 10 literal and inferential questions. The students were required to use information not stated explicitly in the text to answer the questions. Instruction improved literal and inferential comprehension of poor readers but not of good readers.

Dewitz, Carr, and Patberg (1987) used a cloze procedure to teach fifth-grade students to integrate prior knowledge with material that they read. The students were taught to differentiate cloze questions that required use of prior knowledge from cloze questions that could be answered by using clues in the text. For example, if given only the sentence, "The car skidded out of control, and crashed through the railing over the _____ (p.106). The students had to learn that the only way to answer this question was to use their prior knowledge.

After practicing with single sentences, the children were given social studies paragraphs with blanks inserted and had to use clues in the text or their prior knowledge to complete the sentences. Students were taught to distinguish between forward and backward clues. A forward clue is information that occurs after the blank that can be used to answer the inferential question (blank) and a backward clue is one which was read prior to encountering the blank. The students were given feedback regarding their cloze answers and the teacher asked inferential questions based on the text. The final step in the process included transferring the procedure to intact social studies textbook passages by having students use their prior knowledge and clues in the text to answer inferential questions. Throughout instruction, students were provided the following list of questions to aid them in answering the cloze and inferential questions:

(1) Does the answer make sense?
(2) Does the answer make sense in the sentence?
(3) Is the answer based on a combination of knowledge you had before you read the passage and the clues in the passage?
(4) Is there a forward clue in the same sentence, paragraph, or passage?
(5) Is there a backward clue in the same sentence, paragraph, or passage?
(6) Did the clue make you change your answer, or is your answer the same?

Overall, the results of this study showed a positive effect of the cloze instruction on tests of literal and inferential comprehension. In addition, below-average readers tended to benefit more from the instruction than did average or above-average readers.

Activation of prior knowledge is especially recommended for poor readers who may not spontaneously relate their previous experience or knowledge to reading passages. Discussion of prior knowledge seems to be an effective way to increase the knowledge base of all readers in a classroom, given that many readers may not have well-developed knowledge bases relevant to topics in many classroom readings. Although activating prior knowledge seems to have a relatively small effect on reading comprehension, it might improve children's question-answering strategies in that it heightens children's awareness of where to find answers to questions (see discussion of question-answering strategies, this chapter). As a final note of caution, some researchers have found that if text is incompatible with children's prior knowledge, activating that prior knowledge can actually be detrimental to children's comprehension (Lipson, 1982; Smith, Readence, & Alvermann, 1984). Teachers should probably attend to and attempt to correct errors in children's prior knowledge that may be incompatible with information presented in text while they are encouraging activation of prior knowledge.

Concluding Remarks

Students who learned to use all the strategies discussed here would be strategic before, during, and after reading. They would activate their prior knowledge of a topic before reading a passage on that topic and they would generate predictions about text content. During reading, they would construct the gist of what they were reading, either by extracting story-grammar elements of narrative text, or by creating a summary of expository text. They would construct mental images, directly representing concrete content of text or mnemonically encoding more difficult-to-remember content. After reading, they would generate questions to test their memory of the content. They would also look back to appropriate passages of the text to find answers to self-generated or adjunct questions for which they did not recall the answers.

Students who use these strategies should remember more of the text because they would have constructed a rich representation of text while performing the activities. Of course, not all students will benefit from instruction of all of these strategies. It appears that poor readers benefit more from story-grammar training, question-answering strategies, and activation of prior knowledge than do good readers. However, both good and poor readers seem to benefit from summarization, question generation, and mental imagery instruction. Thus, we are optimistic that all teachers can find something useful in the recommendations in this chapter. Reading strategy instruction is not just for remedial readers.

REFERENCES

Anderson, R., & Biddle, W. (1975). On asking people questions about what they are reading. In G.H. Bower (Ed.), *The psychology of learning and motivation*, Vol. 9 (pp.90-132). New York, NY: Academic Press.

Anderson, R.C., Reynolds, R.E., Schallert, D.L., & Goetz, E.T.(1977). Frameworks for comprehending discourse. *American Educational Research Journal*, 14, 367-381.

Armbruster, B.B., Anderson, T.H., & Ostertag, J. (1987). Does text structure/ summarization instruction facilitate learning from expository text? *Reading Research Quarterly*, 22, 331-346.

Baumann, J.E. (1984). The effectiveness of a direct instruction paradigm for teaching main idea comprehension. *Reading Research Quarterly*, 20, 93-115.

Bean, T.W., & Steenwyk, F.L. (1984). The effect of three forms of summarization instruction on sixth graders' summary writing and comprehension. *Journal of Reading Behavior*, 16, 297-306.

Berkowitz, S.J. (1986). Effects of instruction in text organization on sixth-grade students' memory for expository reading. *Reading Research Quarterly*, 21, 161-178.

Beuhring, T., & Kee, D.W. (1987). Developmental relationships among metamemory, elaborative strategy use, and associative memory. *Journal of Experimental Child Psychology*, 44, 377-400.

Bransford, J.D., & Johnson, M.K. (1973). Considerations of some problems of comprehension. In W.G. Chase (Ed.), *Visual information processing*. New York: Academic Press.

Brown, A.L., & Day, J.D. (1983). Macrorules for summarizing texts: The development of expertise. *Journal of Verbal Learning and Verbal Behavior*, 22, 1-14.

Brown, A.L., Day, J.D., & Jones, R.S. (1983). The development of plans for summarizing texts. *Child Development*, 54, 968-979.

Chiesi, H.L., Spilich, G.J., & Voss, J.F. (1979). Acquisition of domain-related information in relation to high and low domain knowledge. *Journal of Verbal Learning and Verbal Behavior*, 18, 257-274.

Davey, B., & McBride, S. (1986). The effects of question generation training on reading comprehension. *Journal of Educational Psychology*, 78, 256-262.

Denner, P.R., & Rickards, J.P. (1987). A developmental comparison of the effects of provided and generated questions on text recall. *Contemporary Educational Psychology*, 12, 135-146.

Dewitz, P., Carr, E.M., & Patberg, J.P. (1987). Effects of inference training on comprehension and comprehension monitoring. *Reading Research Quarterly*, 22, 99-121.

Doctorow, M., Wittrock, M.C., & Marks, C. (1978). Generative processes in reading comprehension. *Journal of Educational Psychology*, 70, 109-118.

Dreher, M.J., & Singer, H. (1980). Story grammar instruction unnecessary for intermediate grade students. *The Reading Teacher*, 33, 261-268.

Gambrell, L.B., & Bales, R.J. (1986). Mental imagery and the comprehension-monitoring performance of fourth- and fifth-grade poor readers. *Reading Research Quarterly*, 21, 454-464.

Garner, R., Hare, V., Alexander, P., V.C., Haynes, J., & Winograd, P. (1984). Inducing use of a text lookback strategy among unsuccessful readers. *American Educational Research Journal*, 21, 789-798.

Garner, R., McCready, G.B., & Wagoner, S. (1984). Readers' acquisition of the components of the text lookback strategy. *Journal of Educational Psychology*, 76, 300-309.

Hansen, J., & Pearson, P.D. (1983). An instructional study: Improving the inferential comprehension of good and poor fourth-grade readers. *Journal of Educational Psychology*, 75, 821-829.

Idol, L. (1987). Group story mapping: A comprehension strategy for both skilled and unskilled readers. *Journal of Learning Disabilities*, 20, 196-205.

Idol, L., & Croll, V.J. (1987). Story-mapping training as a means of improving reading comprehension. *Learning Disability Quarterly*, 10, 214-229.

Jenkins, J.R., Heliotis, J.D., Stein, M.L., & Haynes, M.C. (1987). Improving reading comprehension using paragraph restatements. *Exceptional Children*, 54, 54-59.

Kintsch, W., & van Dijk, T.A. (1978). Toward a model of text comprehension and production. *Psychological Review*, 85, 363-394.

Levin, J.R., & Pressley, M. (1981). Improving childrens' prose comprehension: Selected strategies that seem to succeed. In C.M. Santa & B.L. Hayes (Eds.), *Children's prose comprehension: Research and practice* (pp. 44-71). Newark, DE: International Reading Association.

Levin, J.R., Shriberg, L.K., & Berry, J.K. (1983). A concrete strategy for remembering abstract prose. *American Educational Research Journal*, 20, 277-290.

Lipson, M.Y. (1982). Learning new information from text; The role of prior knowledge and reading ability. *Journal of Reading Behavior*, 14, 243-261.

Mandler, J.M. (1984). *Stories, scripts, and scenes: Aspects of schema theory.* Hillsdale, NJ: Lawrence Erlbaum Associates.

Markman, E.M. (1981). Comprehension monitoring. In W.P. Dickson (Ed.), *Children's oral communication skills* (pp.61-84). New York, NY: Academic Press.

McCormick, C.B., & Levin, J.R. (1984). A comparison of different prose-learning variations of the mnemonic keyword method. *American Educational Research Journal*, 21, 379-398.

McDonald, J.D. (1986). Self-generated questions and reading recall: Does training help? *Contemporary Educational Psychology*, 11, 290-304.

Nolte, R.Y., & Singer, H. (1985). Active comprehension: Teaching a process of reading comprehension and its effects on reading achievement. *The Reading Teacher*, 39, 24-31.

Paivio, A. (1971). *Imagery and verbal processes.* New York, NY: Holt, Rinehart, and Winston Co.

Palincsar, A.M., & Brown, A.L. (1984). Reciprocal teaching of comprehension fostering and comprehension monitoring activities. *Cognition and Instruction*, 1, 117-175.

Paris, S.G., & Lindauer, B.K. (1976). The role of inference in children's comprehension and memory. *Cognitive Psychology*, 8, 217-227.

Pearson, P.D., Hansen, J., & Gordon, C. (1979). The effect of background knowledge on young children's comprehension of explicit and implicit information. *Journal of Reading Behavior*, 11, 201-209.

Peters, E.E., & Levin, J.R. (1986). Effects of a mnemonic imagery strategy on good and poor readers' prose recall. *Reading Research Quarterly, 21,* 179-192.

Pierce, J.W. (1980). Field independence and imagery-assisted prose recall of children. *Journal of Educational Psychology, 72,* 200-203.

Pressley, G.M. (1976). Mental imagery helps eight-year-olds remember what they read. *Journal of Educational Psychology, 68,* 355-359.

Pressley, M. (1977). Imagery and children's learning: Putting the picture in developmental perspective. *Review of Educational Research, 47,* 586-622.

Pressley, M., & Forrest-Pressley, D.L. (1985). Questions and children's cognitive processing. In A.C. Graesser & J.B. Black (Eds.), *The psychology of questions* (pp.277-296). Hillsdale, NJ: Lawrence Erlbaum Associates.

Rahman, T., & Bisanz, G.L. (1986). Reading ability and the use of a story schema in recalling and reconstructing information. *Journal of Educational Psychology, 78,* 323-333.

Raphael, T.E., & McKinney, J. (1983). An examination of fifth- and eighth-grade children's question-answering behavior: An instructional study in metacognition. *Journal of Reading Behavior, 15,* 67-86.

Raphael, T.E., & Pearson, P.D. (1985). Increasing students' awareness of sources of information for answering questions. *American Educational Research Journal, 22,* 217-236.

Raphael, T.E., & Wonnacott, C.A. (1985). Metacognitive training in question-answering strategies: Implementation in a fourth-grade developmental reading program. *Reading Research Quarterly, 20,* 282-296.

Rinehart, S.D., Stahl, S.A., & Erickson, L.G. (1986). Some effects of summarization training on reading and studying. *Reading Research Quarterly, 21,* 422-438.

Rowls, M:D. (1976). The facilitative and interactive effects of adjunct questions on retention of eighth graders across three prose passages: Dissertation in prose learning. *Journal of Educational Psychology, 68,* 205-209.

Sadoski, M. (1983). An exploratory study of the relationship between reported imagery and the comprehension and recall of a story. *Reading Research Quarterly, 19,* 110-123.

Sadoski, M. (1985). The natural use of imagery in story comprehension and recall: Replication and extension. *Reading Research Quarterly*, 20, 658-667.

Short, E.J., & Ryan, E.B. (1984). Metacognitive differences between skilled and less skilled readers: Remediating deficits through story grammar and attribution training. *Journal of Educational Psychology*, 76, 225-235.

Shriberg, L.K., Levin, J.R., McCormick, C.B., & Pressley, M.(1982). Learning about "famous" people via the keyword method. *Journal of Educational Psychology*, 74, 238-247.

Singer, H., & Donlan, D. (1982). Active comprehension: Problem-solving schema with question generation for comprehension of complex short stories. *Reading Research Quarterly*, 17, 166-186.

Smith, L.C., Readence, J.E., & Alvermann, D.E. (1984). Effects of activating background knowledge on comprehension of expository prose. *33rd Yearbook of the National Reading Conference*. Rochester, NY: National Reading Conference.

Stein, N.L., & Glenn, C.G. (1979). An analysis of story comprehension in elementary school children. In R.O. Freedle (Ed.), *New directions in discourse processing* (pp.53-120). Norwood, NJ: Ablex.

Taylor, B.M. (1982). Text structure and children's comprehension and memory for expository material. *Journal of Educational Psychology*, 74, 323-340.

Taylor, B.M., & Beach, R.W. (1984). The effects of text structure instruction on middle-grade students' comprehension and production of expository text. *Reading Research Quarterly*, 19, 134-146.

Wilson, P.T., & Anderson, R.C. (1986). What they don't know will hurt them: The role of prior knowledge in comprehension. In J. Orasanu (Ed.), *Reading comprehension: From research to practice*. Hillsdale, NJ: Lawrence Erlbaum Associates.

Wong, B.Y.L., (1985). Self-questioning instructional research: A review. *Review of Educational Research*, 55, 227-268.

CHAPTER 4

Vocabulary

The following statement, two decades old, represents an almost universal attitude toward vocabulary held both by educators and those outside the field today:

> The importance of vocabulary is daily demonstrated in schools and out. In the classroom, the achieving students possess the most adequate vocabularies. Because of the verbal nature of most classroom activities, knowledge of words and ability to use language are essential to success in these activities. After schooling has ended, adequacy of vocabulary is almost equally essential for achievement in vocations and in society (Petty, Harold, & Stoll, 1968, p. 7).

More specifically, vocabulary has been found to be important to text comprehension (Anderson & Freebody, 1981). Since text comprehension is an ultimate goal of reading, some reading instructional time should be devoted to vocabulary development.

Vocabulary Instruction in Schools

Although vocabulary instruction appears to be a key element in education, there is very little research examining the vocabulary instruction currently taking place in schools. When researchers have looked, however, they have found little teaching of vocabulary learning strategies. In one analysis of basal readers, Beck, Perfetti & McKeown (1982) examined vocabulary instruction presented in two third-grade through sixth-grade basal reading books, dividing their attention between pre-reading activities, during-reading activities, and post-reading activities. One basal series included no pre-reading activities; the other included words taught in sentences specifically designed to reveal their meaning. Both series assumed that students obtain meanings from natural contexts, contexts during reading, and failed to suggest effective teaching strategies. Students were also taught to look up words in the glossary. One series presented a set of words not previously taught for post-reading instruction; the other provided one review of the new words in the selection.

In a study of comprehension instruction in fourth grade classrooms, Durkin (1979-80), observed a total of 4,469 minutes of instruction. Durkin found that only 19 minutes were devoted to vocabulary instruction, with an additional 4 minutes devoted to vocabulary review. In short, little time was spent on teaching of vocabulary at all.

Shake, Allington, Gaskins, and Marr (1987) reported similar results. Twenty teachers were asked to present an exemplary vocabulary lesson. Although all teachers provided definitions and taught strategies on using context and semantic features (i.e., focussing on conceptual development), most instruction provided very few opportunities for students to use the words they were learning. Often there was a misunderstanding of the task requested by the teacher evident in the response supplied by the student. For example, one teacher said, "Use 'harpoon' in a sentence." The student's response was: "Well, it's long and sharp and used to kill whales." In summary, it seems reasonable to conclude that the vocabulary instruction that students receive in schools is quite meager.

What Should Be Taught?

Carr and Wixson (1986) advocate that vocabulary instruction should develop students' strategies for independently acquiring new vocabulary. Because of the enormous number of words the mature reader needs to understand, it is important for students to learn how to acquire the meanings of new words. Students become independent learners through instruction that gradually shifts the responsibility of developing new word meanings from the teacher to the student. Students need to develop methods by which they can acquire word meanings, learn how to monitor their understanding of new vocabulary, and change or modify current strategies when they cannot infer from them the meanings of new words. While a number of strategies to accomplish these goals have been suggested by educators, few of them have empirical support. These include opposition (Powell, 1986), which consists of presenting children opposites or antonymns of to-be-learned vocabulary words; self-collection (Haggard, 1986), composed of student-generated word lists; and looking at cartoons (Goldstein, 1986). In contrast, the keyword method and some internal contextual approaches reviewed in this chapter have received a good deal of research attention and empirical support.

The Keyword Method [T & SSR]

The keyword method is a mnemonic technique based on mental imagery which can facilitate associative aspects of learning such as learning associations between new vocabulary and their meanings (Bower, 1972; Paivio, 1971). It was originally developed for learning foreign language vocabularies (Atkinson, 1975; Atkinson & Raugh, 1975: Raugh & Atkinson, 1975), but has since been successfully adapted to acquisition of first-language vocabulary (Levin, 1981).

The keyword method consists of two stages, an "acoustic-link" stage and an "imagery-link" stage (Pressley, Levin, & McDaniel, 1987). In the acoustic-link stage, the individual acquires a "keyword," which is a familiar English word (assuming that the student's first language is English) that (a) sounds like a salient part of the unfamiliar word and (b) is visualizable through a mental image. In the imagery-link stage, the learner forms a visual image in which the keyword and the definition interact (see Table 4-1).

A few examples from Spanish illustrate the keyword method. In Span-

---

Table 4-1
Stages of the Keyword Method

Take an unfamiliar word.

For example, "persuade" and "surplus" are unfamiliar words that one may want fourth grade students to know.

Acquire a familiar English word as a keyword.

Keywords should:
    a) sound like a salient part of the unfamiliar word, and
    b) be readily visualizable through a mental image

For example, "purse" is a suitable keyword for "persuade" while "syrup" is an appropriate keyword for "surplus."

Form a link between keyword and unknown word.

Students should be instructed to associate the keyword and the unfamiliar word by visualizing them interacting.

Using the example of "persuade" as the unfamiliar word and "purse" as the selected keyword, one may form a picture of a woman being persuaded to buy a purse.

Similarly, using the example of "surplus" as the unfamiliar word and "syrup" as the selected keyword, one may form a picture of a boy pouring a lot of syrup on pancakes because there is a surplus of it in the cupboard.

Examples cited in Pressley, Levin, & McDaniel (1987)

ish the word *caballo* means horse. The pronounciation of the Spanish word contains a sound that resembles the English word *eye*. Employing the English word eye as the keyword, one might form a mental image of a cyclopean eye in the forehead of a mythical horse or, alternatively, a horse rearing up and kicking at a giant eye. As another example, the Spanish word for duck is *pato*. Using the English word *pot* as the keyword, one could imagine a duck hiding under an overturned flower pot, with its webbed feet and tufted tail sticking out below.

The keyword method has a solid foundation in learning theory. Psychological "principles" drawn upon by the keyword method are that (a) meaningful stimuli are far more reliably encoded than nonmeaningful stimuli; (b) interacting items are more reliably associated than noninteracting items; (c) the greater the similarity between two stimuli, the more reliably one will evoke the other; and (d) thematic interactions are reliably retrieved from appropriate cues (Levin, 1981).

The keyword method has been empirically tested with grade-school children in many studies by Levin, Pressley, and their colleagues (Levin et al., 1982; Levin et al., 1979; Pressley & Levin, 1978; Pressley, Levin, & Delaney, 1982). The method has been compared both to control conditions in which no explicit instruction is given and to several variants of the learning-from-context method. The keyword method has always proven to be at least as effective as, and usually more effective than, the alternative methods against which it has been compared.

For example, in a study with fourth- and fifth-grade children, Levin et al. (1984) compared two groups of children, one receiving the mnemonic keyword method and the other group receiving a contextual-analysis strategy. The contextual-analysis strategy required that students search for clues contained in short paragraphs, clues that supposedly enable unfamiliar word meanings to be inferred. For example, the following passage was used to provide contextual support for the word *angler* (a person who likes to go fishing):

> The *angler* carried a lot of things down to the stream. He carried a net and a tackle box, as well as his fishing pole. He hoped to catch a lot of fish that afternoon.

The experimenter pointed out the specific fishing and fisherman-related words within the paragraph (e.g., stream, he [to signify that an angler is a person], fishing pole) that could furnish clues for deducing and confirming the word's meaning. Children who were assigned to the keyword condition were introduced to the word *angler* via an illustration in which an angel (a keyword for *angler*) was depicted fishing.

Students who were provided with keyword illustrations remembered about 50% more when required to recall the definitions given the vocabulary words than did students in the contextual analysis condition. This held for both high and low-achievers [Levin et al. (1984)].

In another study, Pressley, Ross, Levin, and Ghatala (1984) demonstrated that the keyword mnemonic was superior to another contextual approach frequently used in schools. Ten- to 13-year-olds were presented a list of 22 low-frequency English nouns and their definitions. Half of the items were studied via the keyword method, and half were studied by constructing sentence contexts with the target words used appropriately. After one learning trial, the keyword method advantage was substantial: definitions of 51% of the keyword items were recalled in contrast to 8.5% of the context definitions. Definition recall of keyword items exceeded that of context items for 93% of the children.

Pressley, Levin and their associates have provided ample documentation that effective keyword mnemonic interventions can be engineered (e.g., Pressley, Samuel, Hershey, Bishop & Dickinson, 1981), although it is not until the late grade-school years that children are able to generate keyword images proficiently, if given the vocabulary words, keywords, and definitions (Pressley & Levin, 1978). Positive keyword benefits are not limited to normal populations either. Pressley, Levin, and McDaniel (1987) summarized the evidence that the keyword method can promote vocabulary learning in poor learners, including learning disabled students (e.g. Mastropieri, Scruggs, & Levin, 1985), low verbal ability children (McGivern & Levin, 1983), and mentally retarded children (Scruggs, Matropieri, & Levin, 1985).

The method is adaptable to materials possessing diverse characteristics. Children can use the method to learn verbs, abstract nouns, and adjectives (Levin, McCormick, Miller, Berry, and Pressley, 1982). Levin et al. (1982) used words provided by the editor of a national children's magazine—ones not selected for keyword-method compatibility (e.g., easy-to-generate keywords). The fourth-grade students in that study learned items like *persuade, hesitate, sect,* and *intend,* achieving much better learning in comparison to fourth-grade students in a no-strategy condition.

Michael Gruneberg has published several books to aid students in learning a foreign language, each based on the "link word" system, a mental imagery approach much like the keyword method.[1] Students are presented with a word and its definition: "The Spanish for *cat* is *gato.*" Students are to form an image between the definition and a word which sounds like the new word. For example, they may be asked, "Imagine a *cat* eating a lovely *gateau.*" They are told to think of the image for about ten seconds before moving on to the next word. For example, for the German word *nur,* which means *only,* Gruneberg suggested imagining thinking "If I only knew her," a sentence including the meaning and a phrase acoustically similar to the to-be-learned item (i.e., "knew her" for *nur*). Although there are only preliminary data to support this method, (Gruneberg, Nov. 1987, personal communication to M. Pressley) it is provisionally recommended because it is based on the same principle as the keyword method. On the face of it, Gruneberg's books should be helpful from the late grade-school years on, a proposition that deserves serious scientific study, given that these books are being disseminated widely.

Unfortunately, the number of words students need to learn is great. Nagy and Anderson (1984) estimate that the number of distinct words in printed school English is between 54,000 and 88,500, a number simply too large for classroom instruction. In contrast, a direct vocabulary teaching program typically includes 10 to 12 words a week, or about 400 a year.

It therefore seems inadvisable to teach only strategies that are part of direct instruction, such as the keyword method. It is also important to prepare students to be able to learn vocabulary from semantic context.

Learning from Context

In typical studies of learning from context, students are presented several sentences that include the to-be-learned word in ways that can elucidate its meaning (Jenkins & Dixon, 1983) [T]. The individual is required to infer the word's meaning, and may be asked to use the word in a sentence that shows comprehension of the meaning but is different from the given sentences. An example of this approach is given by Gipe (1979) for the word "barbarian":

> The *barbarian* kicked the dog and hit the owner in the nose. Any person who acts mean to anybody or to anything is a barbarian. *Barbarian* means a person who is very mean. (p.630)

After reading these sentences, the individual is asked to write something that a barbarian might do at a dinner table. Although this approach is one that has been widely used in schools, it has received very little empirical support (for review, see Pressley, Levin & McDaniel, 1987). Effects that have been reported have been small and not replicable (e.g. Gipe, 1979, 1981; Sternberg & Powell, 1983; Sternberg, 1987).

A more promising contextual approach is one that teaches students how to derive word meanings by examining their internal contextual features [*SSR*]. Students can be taught about the usefulness of internal cues in deciphering the meaning of unknown words. Suppose the task is to infer the meaning of the word "dissimilarity." The word is probably unfamiliar to most young children. But many children know that the prefix *"dis"* refers to *not*, that the root "similar" is a word meaning *"the same as,"* and that the suffix *"ity"* is often used to form abstract nouns. These cues might be combined to infer that *"dissimilarity"* refers to the property of not being the same as. This inference would be correct.

There have been several studies of morphological instruction. Graves and Hammond (1980) taught seventh graders nine prefixes over a three-day period. There were reliable differences between the group taught the prefixes and a control group on a test of the prefixes taught and on a transfer test requiring students to use their knowledge of the prefixes taught to infer the meanings of novel words containing the prefixes. These results were obtained both immediately following teaching and three weeks after instruction had ended. In a related study, Nicol, Graves and Slater (1984) found similar results with fourth, fifth, and sixth graders of high, middle, and low ability.

Pressley, Levin, Woo, Sinclair, and Ahmad (1985) provided elementary-school students with mastery-learning instruction (i.e., to study until they are 100% correct) of some root words. Students learned roots such as *dorm*, meaning "sleep," *chrom*, meaning "color," and *taph*, meaning "tomb." When later asked to remember that *dormeuse* means "a sleeping carriage," that *chromatosis* means an "unnatural coloring of the skin," and that *cenotaph* means "a monument to a person buried elsewhere," these internal-context mastery subjects were far superior to control subjects who were not given the previous internal-context instruction. Such a finding suggests that remembering new vocabulary can be facilitated through students' capitalizing on previously learned word parts.

One way of teaching meaning from word parts is to teach words together as a family. This approach has a number of advantages. First, if the most frequent words in the family are already known, this procedure builds a bridge from familiar to new. What additional time is devoted to the derivatives would also function to reinforce the learning of the base word. In addition, covering a family of words would familiarize students with the types of changes in meanings that often occur between related words.

Concluding Comments

Mnemonic and internal-contextual approaches are complementary. Learners can derive vocabulary meanings from internal context but this process doesn't foster retention of specific definitional meanings. Mnemonic techniques positively affect remembering, but do not permit learners to infer the meanings of undefined vocabulary words (Pressley, Levin & McDaniel, 1987). How learning from internal context compares with more direct vocabulary instruction depends entirely upon the type of comparison that is made. If the goal is to teach the meanings of a small number of words in a short amount of time, then some form of direct, word-by-word instruction (e.g., the keyword method) will be most efficient. However, if the goal is development of students who can derive tacit knowledge of a large number of words (i.e., a general idea of the meaning of the word while reading), then an internal contextual approach should be more beneficial.

Note

1. Although the actual texts are not yet available in North America, the materials can be obtained on microdisks from Artworx, Inc., 1844 Penfield Road, Penfield, N.Y. Phone: (716) 385-6120.

REFERENCES

Anderson, R.C., & Freebody, P. (1981). Vocabulary knowledge. In J.T. Guthrie (Ed.), *Comprehension and teaching: Research reviews*. Newark, DE: International Reading Association.

Atkinson, R.C. (1975). Mnemotechnics in second-language learning. *American Psychologist, 30*, 821-828.

Atkinson, R.C., & Raugh, M.R. (1975). An application of the mnemonic keyword method to the acquisition of a Russian vocabulary. *Journal of Experimental Psychology: Human Learning and Memory*, 123-133.

Beck, I.L., Perfetti, C.A., & McKeown, M.O. (1982). The effects of long-term vocabulary instruction on lexical access and reading comprehension. *Journal of Educational Psychology, 74*, 506-521.

Bower, O.H. (1972). Mental imagery and associative learning. In L.W. Gregg (Ed.), *Cognition in learning and memory*. New York: John Wiley & Sons.

Carr, E., & Wixson, K.K. (1986). Guidelines for evaluating vocabulary instruction. *Journal of Reading, 29*, 588-595.

Durkin, D. (1978-79). What classroom observations reveal about reading comprehension instruction. *Reading Research Quarterly, 14*, 481-533.

Gipe, J.P. (1979). Investigating techniques for teaching word meanings. *Reading Research Quarterly, 14*, 624-644.

Gipe, J. (1981). *Investigation of techniques for teaching new word meanings*. Paper presented at the annual meeting of the American Educational Research Association, Los Angeles, April.

Goldstein, B.S. (1986). Looking at cartoons and comics in a new way. *Journal of Reading, 29*, 657-661.

Graves, M.F., & Hammond, H.K. (1980). A validated procedure for teaching prefixes and its effect on students' ability to assign meaning to novel words. In M.L. Kamil & A.V. Moe (Eds.), *Perspectives on reading research and instruction*. Washington, DC: National Reading Conference.

Haggard, M.R. (1986). Teaching vocabulary through opposition. *Journal of Reading, 29*, 617-621.

Jenkins, J.R., & Dixon, R. (1983). Vocabulary learning. *Contemporary Educational Psychology, 8*, 237-280.

Levin, J.R. (1981). The mnemonic '80s: Keywords in the classroom. *Educational Psychologist, 16*, 65-82.

Levin, J.R., Johnson, D.D., Pittelman, S.D., Hayes, B.L., Levin, K.M., Shriberg, L.K., & Toms-Bronowski, S. (1984). A comparison of semantic- and mnemonic-based vocabulary-learning strategies. *Reading Psychology, 5*, 1-15.

Levin, J.R., McCormick, C.B., Miller, G.E., Berry J.K., & Pressley, M. (1982). Mnemonic versus non-mnemonic vocabulary-learning strategies for children. *American Educational Research Journal, 19*, 121-136.

Levin, J.R., Pressley, M., McCormick, C.B., Miller, G.E., & Shriberg, L.K. (1979). Assessing the classroom potential of the keyword method. *Journal of Educational Psychology, 71*, 583-594.

Mastropieri, M.A., Scruggs, T.E., & Levin, J.R. (1985). Maximizing what exceptional children can learn: A review of research on the keyword method and related mnemonic techniques. *Remedial and Special Education, 6*, 39-45.

McGivern, J.E., & Levin, J.R. (1983). The keyword method and children's vocabulary learning: An interaction with vocabulary knowledge. *Contemporary Educational Psychology, 8*, 46-54.

Nagy, W., & Anderson, R. (1984). The number of words in printed school English. *Reading Research Quarterly, 19*, 304-330.

Nicol, J.E., Graves, M.F., & Slater, W.H. (1984). *Building vocabulary through prefix instruction*. Unpublished manuscript, University of Minnesota.

Paivio, A. (1971). *Imagery and verbal processes*. New York: Henry Holt.

Petty, W., Harold, C., & Stoll, E. (1968). *The state of knowledge about the teaching of vocabulary*. Champaign, IL: National Council of Teachers of English.

Powell, W.R. (1986). Teaching vocabulary through opposition. *Journal of Reading, 29*, 617-621.

Pressley, M., & Levin, J.R. (1978). Developmental constraints associated with children's use of the keyword method of foreign language vocabulary learning. *Journal of Educational Psychology, 26*, 359-372.

Pressley, M., Levin, J.R., & Delaney, H.D. (1982). The mnemonic keyword method. *Review of Educational Research, 52*, 61-92.

Pressley, M., Levin, J.R., & McDaniel, M.A. (1987). Remembering versus inferring what a word means: mnemonic and contextual approaches. In M.O. McKeown & M.E. Curtis (Eds.), *The nature of vocabulary acquisition*. Hillsdale, NJ: Lawrence Erlbaum Associates.

Pressley, M., Levin, J.R., Woo, G., Sinclair, C., & Ahmad, F. (1985). *The effect of root-word mastery on vocabulary learning*. Unpublished manuscript. University of Western Ontario, London, Ontario.

Pressley, M., Ross, K.A., Levin, J.R., & Ghatala, E.S. (1984). The role of strategy utility knowledge in children's strategy decision making. *Journal of Experimental Child Psychology, 38*, 491-504.

Pressley, M., Samuel, J., Hershey, M.M., Bishop, S.L., & Dickinson, D. (1981). Use of a mnemonic technique to teach young children foreign language vocabulary. *Contemporary Educational Psychology, 6*, 110-116.

Raugh, M.R., & Atkinson, R.C. (1975). A mnemonic method for learning a second-language vocabulary. *Journal of Educational Psychology, 67*, 1-16.

Scruggs, T.E., Mastropieri, M.A., & Levin, J.R. (1985). Vocabulary acquisition of retarded students under direct and mnemonic instruction. *American Journal of Mental Deficiency, 89*, 546-551.

Shake, M.C., Allington, R.L., Gaskins, R., & Marr, M.B. (1987). *How teachers teach vocabulary*. Paper presented to the National Reading Conference.

Sternberg, R.J. (1987). Most vocabulary is learned from context. In M.G. McKeown & M.E. Curtis (Eds.), *Nature of vocabulary acquisition*. Hillsdale, NJ: Lawrence Erlbaum Associates.

Sternberg, R.J., & Powell, J.S. (1983). Comprehending verbal comprehension. *American Psychologist, 38*, 878-893.

CHAPTER 5

Spelling

Correct spelling is often associated with educational attainment, accuracy, neatness, and cultivation. Spelling inability, on the other hand, is often associated with illiteracy, and may adversely affect a person's occupational status (Allred, 1984; Graham & Miller, 1979; Weisberg, 1985). There is a lot of motivation to spell well, an ambition that is within reach because good spelling requires a relatively small amount of learning. Spelling vocabularies between 2,800 and 3,000 words are sufficient for fluent and intelligent communication in both children and adults (Fitzgerald, 1951a; Graham, 1983; Horn, 1926, 1967; Rinsland, 1945; Thomas, 1972). For example, about 50 words accounted for almost half (49%) of the words that elementary-grade children use in writing (Thomas, 1979). Five hundred words accounted for 80% of the words used in written communication; 1,000 words for 86%; 2,000 words for 92%; and 3,000 words for 95%. A surprisingly small number of words (approximately 300) account for more than half the words children misspell in their writing (Allred, 1984; Thomas, 1979).

How do children obtain such spelling vocabularies? Although the exact mechanisms by which children acquire spelling knowledge are still unknown (and probably vary across individuals), we do know that spelling skills develop in an orderly fashion in most children, even handicapped students (Hall, 1984). Researchers have documented three basic stages or types of spelling errors evidenced by the majority of children as they develop spelling competence, with these errors occurring in a particular developmental order.

In the first stage, known as the prephonetic stage, the child's spelling attempts consist of only one or two salient letter sounds, usually the beginning or ending consonants. Prephonetic stage spellers use phoneme-grapheme relations, or sound-letter patterns, to spell (Drake & Ehri, 1984). For example, the letters "HKN" might be used to represent the word "chicken." Prephonetic spellers are typically in kindergarten or grade 1, know their letters, and are just beginning to read and spell (Zutell, 1979).

Stage 2 spellers, or phonetic spellers, adopt a sequential sounding-out strategy and represent individually articulated sounds with letters that share acoustic similarity (e.g., FET = feet, TABL = table). These children will master the majority of phoneme-grapheme relationships, and are developing and improving their ability to segment pronunciations into sequences of phoneme patterns. Typically, stage 2 spellers are either late grade 1 or grade

2 readers (Zutell, 1979).

The third stage, known as the transitional stage, is characterized by attempts to replace phonetic spellings with conditional letter patterns and/or morpheme (meaning) spelling patterns. The transitional speller has abandoned the belief that one letter is required for every sound (Drake & Ehri, 1984). For instance, to represent the word "watched" the transitional speller might spell "woched." Children usually reach the transitional stage after the second grade.

Some researchers (Beers & Henderson, 1977; Henderson & Beers, 1980) believe there is a fourth stage, characterized by the acquisition of correct spellings. However, this can only be considered a relative stage since children may be able to spell some words correctly (e.g., frequently seen words), but not others. For instance, phonetic-stage spellers may spell "looked" correctly because they have frequently encountered the word and have subsequently memorized it (Drake & Ehri, 1984). On the other hand, the same children may misspell the less familiar word "watched" as "wocht."

Children's perceptions of spelling ability are not consistent with this sequence of developmental improvement. Downing, DeStefano, Rich, and Bell (1985) investigated the spelling perceptions of students across the first to sixth grades. From grade two onward, children's perceptions of themselves as good spellers declined. For instance, by grade three, less than half the students interviewed considered themselves to be "good spellers." When asked why some children spell poorly, many children responded that poor spelling resulted from the lack of study and/or practice, or that poor spelling was precipitated by a failure to pay attention to the teacher during class. Other children, especially those in grade three, were particularly reluctant to discuss this topic. Although the majority of the children felt spelling was an important skill, many children reported negative emotions associated with spelling instruction. The authors found that the spelling strategy most frequently used by these children in everyday writing situations involved the analysis of words according to their phonetic units (i.e., spelling words by sounding them out). The authors concluded that most children overemphasized the importance of phoneme-grapheme relations.

Radebaugh (1985) studied 17 children in the third and fourth grades. Based on spelling tests and teachers' judgments, nine of these children were considered to be poor spellers, while the other eight were good spellers. Each child was asked to elaborate on the tactics he/she would use when spelling two easy-to-spell words (words whose spellings were known) and two hard-to-spell words (words whose spellings were unknown). Both good and poor spellers claimed that the spellings of the easy words came automatically. When asked about the specific strategies used to spell these words, good spellers reported being able to visualize the words, while poor spellers relied on sounding the words out.

When children were asked how they would spell the hard words, the poor spellers retained the sounding out strategy. Specifically, these children divided the words into syllabic parts and sounded out each part of the word unit. In other words, the poor spellers used a letter-by-letter phonetic strategy when spelling. For example, one poor speller spelled the word "cautiously" as "koshisle." In contrast, good spellers relied on a variety of spelling strategies to spell the hard words. One strategy reported by good spellers involved breaking the words into units (not necessarily syllables) and trying to visualize how these units looked. For instance, one child reported recalling how she had printed the word "squirrel" on her crayon box earlier in the year (i.e., imagery strategy). Another strategy reported by the good spellers involved breaking the words into smaller parts and using the spelling pattern of a known word as a substitute for the spelling of the unknown word part (i.e., analogy strategy). For example, one child who used the analogy strategy spelled the word dinosaur as "dinosoar." Alternatively, some good spellers reported relying upon memorized spelling rules.

Overall, poor spellers mentioned using fewer strategies than did good spellers. Poor spellers also used more phonetic strategies than did good spellers and did not make use of imagery techniques. Marino (1980) drew similar conclusions concerning the strategies used by good and poor spellers. Marino found that as spellers became more proficient, they became more aware of sound-letter correspondences, but they also became more aware of the many constraints within each correspondence. Good spellers demonstrated awareness of common letter patterns and letter rules. Poor spellers, however, failed to display such knowledge.

Particularly relevant for this chapter on spelling instruction, good spellers reported using techniques (e.g., imagery, analogy) that research has demonstrated to be very effective in promoting spelling. Poor spellers, on the other hand, tended to be overly dependent on using phonetic strategies, strategies that do not seem to promote spelling acquisition to the degree that imagery, analogy, and other nonphonetic strategies do (Yee, 1969).

The Status of Spelling Instruction in the Classroom

Spelling is a mainstay of the elementary school curriculum. Yet many school-aged children have difficulties spelling, particularly those children who are either learning disabled or mentally delayed (Gerber & Lydiatt, 1984). In addition, there is growing concern that today's students are poorer spellers than students of 30 to 40 years ago (Graham & Miller, 1979). Why do children have difficulties acquiring spelling skills? While there does not appear to be any one answer to this question, it is probable that less than adequate teaching materials and instructional techniques may exacerbate students' difficulties.

Almost twenty years ago, Cohen (1969; cited in Graham, 1983) methodically analyzed the contents of popular spelling texts. Many of the texts contained activities that were irrelevant and inappropriate to acquisition of spelling skills. For instance, some texts included exercises that actually interfered with acquisition of spelling patterns, such as activities involving phonetic re-spelling. In addition, the texts rarely allowed students to generate spelling words in response to their own needs.

Today, it still appears that the majority of spelling instruction depends on commercial texts (90% in Cronnell & Humes, 1980). In itself, this is not particularly disturbing. However, Cronnell and Humes also found that the more widely used texts tended to concentrate upon the teaching of individual words and not the teaching of spelling patterns *per se*.

In addition, spelling instruction is not always done efficiently. Over a period of five to eight consecutive visits, Hillerich (1982) observed 34 spelling periods in six elementary school classes (grades 2, 3, 6, 7, and 8). Hillerich found that the majority of teachers devoted approximately 40 minutes per day to spelling activities. This is despite the empirically supported fact that the majority of children do not benefit from more than 60 to 75 minutes of spelling instruction per week (Allred, 1977; Reith et al., 1974). More disturbing, anywhere between 30% to 80% of spelling instruction time was used for irrelevant administrative or instructional activities (disciplining students, giving mechanical directions, grading papers). The correction of spelling workbook exercises was the next most popular activity, an activity not centrally relevant to learning.

Hillerich observed little instruction about how to acquire spelling skills, nor did teachers recommend or model strategies that could be used to study spelling words. In most classes, students were assigned exercises from their workbooks and then graded based on the results of spelling tests. Dictation of these spelling tests comprised between 4% and 18% of the total instructional time. Only one teacher provided students with immediate feedback by correcting the spelling tests orally. The remaining teachers collected the students' work, graded the tests, and handed the results back to students during the next instructional period.

In most classrooms, spelling instruction is based on traditional methods and not empirical research (Graham, 1983). In fact, investigators have found that some empirically supported methods, like presenting to-be-learned spelling words in list form or having students correct their own spelling tests, are rejected by a large number of teachers (Fitzsimmons & Loomer, 1977). The purpose of this chapter is to inform teachers of effective spelling strategies that enjoy empirical support, and provide examples of how these techniques have been successfully implemented in the classroom. The strategies covered are those most appropriate for students at the elementary level. For examples of some strategies appropriate for more mature students, see Hodges (1982) or Templeton (1983).

The discussion of spelling strategies will be divided into four sections. In the first, organizational and instructional hints are presented. These hints are intended to help teachers design effective spelling curricula and maintain students' interest. The second section is devoted to discussion of spelling strategies that are demonstrably useful in the acquisition of spelling skills. These strategies can be used when teaching children how to learn and remember word spellings. Third, effective strategies for correcting spelling are presented. The correction and analysis of spelling errors provides an excellent opportunity for the student to acquire new spelling skills and allows the teacher to monitor students' spelling progress. The fourth section summarizes proofreading tactics designed to help the student detect and correct their own spelling errors.

Organizational and Instructional Hints [T]

Organizational and instructional hints that can enhance the daily instruction of spelling are summarized in Table 5-1. All of these teaching strategies have been shown to enhance spelling instruction (Allred, 1977; Allred, 1984; Graham, 1983; Graham & Miller, 1979; Thomas, 1979). Teachers are encouraged to implement these general recommendations into their daily instructional activities.

Readiness for spelling. Prior to any spelling instruction, the student's readiness for instruction should be assessed. Spelling instruction should only be administered to those children who are able to write and name all the letters of the alphabet. Children should be able to copy words accurately, be able to spell their names correctly, and be able to enunciate words clearly. Children who are prepared for spelling instruction are able to recognize common letter-sound combinations, recognize that words are composed of different letters, ask for words they are in doubt about, write a few words from memory, and are able to express a few thoughts in writing. These children are usually reading at a grade-2 level or better. Finally, but equally important, the child should express some interest in spelling (Allred, 1984; Graham & Miller, 1979). If the child does not display these characteristics, then the child is not a suitable candidate for spelling instruction.

Teachers who encounter students that do not present themselves as ready for formal spelling instruction are referred to a book by Hildreth (1956). In her book, Hildreth outlines activities designed to foster spelling instruction readiness.

Teachers need to impart the importance of spelling in both formal and social communications. To help maintain students' interest and motivation, spelling instruction should concentrate on words that are in the students' present, or near future, listening and reading vocabularies (Thomas, 1979). Teachers should constantly encourage students' spelling attempts, encourage pride in correct spelling, and praise spelling progress. To help maintain students' interest, the occasional use of spelling games such as Masterspeller, Hangman, and Spelling Bingo are recommended (Graham, 1983). However, games should be used to supplement instruction only; they should not substitute for primary instruction. For examples of spelling games and references, see Graham, Freeman, and Miller (1981) and Thomas (1979).

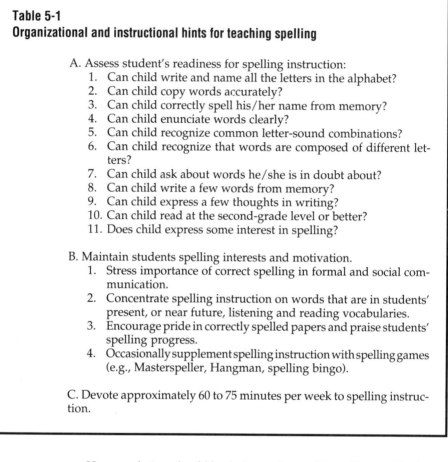

Table 5-1
Organizational and instructional hints for teaching spelling

A. Assess student's readiness for spelling instruction:
1. Can child write and name all the letters in the alphabet?
2. Can child copy words accurately?
3. Can child correctly spell his/her name from memory?
4. Can child enunciate words clearly?
5. Can child recognize common letter-sound combinations?
6. Can child recognize that words are composed of different letters?
7. Can child ask about words he/she is in doubt about?
8. Can child write a few words from memory?
9. Can child express a few thoughts in writing?
10. Can child read at the second-grade level or better?
11. Does child express some interest in spelling?

B. Maintain students spelling interests and motivation.
1. Stress importance of correct spelling in formal and social communication.
2. Concentrate spelling instruction on words that are in students' present, or near future, listening and reading vocabularies.
3. Encourage pride in correctly spelled papers and praise students' spelling progress.
4. Occasionally supplement spelling instruction with spelling games (e.g., Masterspeller, Hangman, spelling bingo).

C. Devote approximately 60 to 75 minutes per week to spelling instruction.

How much time should be designated to spelling? Sixty to 75 minutes per week (approximately 15 minutes per day) is a sufficient amount of time (Allred, 1977; Allred, 1984; Horn, 1960, 1967; Reith, et al., 1974; Thomas, 1979). Short periods of spelling instruction are recommended because there is evidence that extended study periods lower student interest and motivation (Horn, 1960; cited in Thomas, 1979). However, it is important that this is time for promotion of efficient and meaningful spelling activities—students should be allowed to focus on their own special spelling needs. This time should not be devoted to discipline, administrative, or other such activities.

Perhaps one of the greatest controversies regarding effective spelling instruction concerns the use of phonics. *We recommend that teachers limit the*

Table 5-1 (cont.)
Organizational and instructional hints for teaching spelling

D. Limit the use of phonic instruction.

E. Teach spelling rules that apply to a large number of words and have only a few exceptions.

F. Present spelling words in lists rather than in context.

G. Study spelling words as whole units versus syllabified forms.

H. Use the test-study-test method versus the study-test method.
   1. Administer spelling pretest to students.
   2. Spelling instruction concentrates on only those words spelled incorrectly.
   3. Spelling test administered including both words spelled correctly and incorrectly at pretest.

I. Have students monitor their own spelling progress.

J. Individualize spelling instruction.
   1. Be responsive to the unique needs of individual students.
   2. Choose students' spelling materials to match their personal needs.
   3. Plan, monitor and modify spelling instruction according to the needs of the individual student.

K. Teach spelling as part of general language study.

use of phonic instruction when teaching spelling skills. In part, arguments against the use of phonics instruction are derived from the fact that the English language has one of the largest and most complex vocabularies in the world. In English, the 26 letters of the alphabet represent approximately 44 sounds; there are silent letters; there are variant and invariant sounds; and there are 300 different letter combinations that represent 17 vowel sounds. To help place these complexities into perspective, consider that, when spelled phonetically, there are over 396,000,000 different spellings for the word "circumference" (Graham & Miller, 1979).

In comprehensive reviews of the spelling literature, Graham (1983) and Graham and Miller (1979) explain that phonic instruction can be problematic for several reasons. First, most sounds can be spelled more than one way and most letters spell many sounds. Second, many misspellings are phonemically correct. Over one-third of the words in the dictionary have more than one accepted pronunciation but only one correct spelling. More than one half of the words in the dictionary are comprised of silent letters, and one sixth of these words have double letters. In addition, unstressed syllables prove difficult to spell phonetically.

A related argument against the use of phonic instruction originates from the high proportion of phonetic errors committed by students. For example, research carried out in Alberta with 449 fourth- through sixth-grade students revealed that over 50% of a total of 5301 spelling errors involved phonetic substitutions, letter omissions, and errors resulting from inaccurate pronunciations (Thomas, 1979). Further, teachers consistently ranked phonetic substitutions and omissions as the first and second most common type of spelling error committed by students. In addition, research indicates that poor spellers tend to rely upon phonetic strategies, while good spellers use more effective strategies (e.g., Downing et al., 1985; Radebaugh, 1985).

On the other hand, there are researchers who contend that phonic instruction is valuable, considering the regular nature of some sound-symbol relationships (Gillingham & Stillman, 1969; Hanna et al., 1967). Nonetheless, evidence in support of phonics is mixed at best (Cramer, 1969; Block, 1972; Hahn, 1964; Horn, 1969; Ibeling, 1961; Personke & Tee, 1971; Tee, 1969). Therefore, like others (e.g., Allred, 1984; Graham, 1983; Graham & Miller, 1979), *we recommend only the provisional use of phonics instruction and that teachers supplement spelling instruction with other empirically supported strategies.*

Spelling rules. Should children be taught spelling rules? Because of the number of irregularities and exceptions that exist within the English language system, only a limited number of spelling rules have proven valuable to spelling instruction (Blake & Emans, 1970; Graham & Miller, 1979; Thomas, 1979). Specifically, only those rules or generalizations that apply to a large number of words and have only a few exceptions are useful when teaching spelling skills. These rules are listed in Table 5-2. Teachers are reminded, however, that when teaching rules, emphasis needs to be placed on the development and use of the rule and not upon the memorization of the verbal statement (Thomas, 1979). In other words, students need to be provided with practical situations in which they can apply these rules.

The spelling list method. Another common misunderstanding in spelling instruction concerns the utility of the "list method" (i.e., learn a list of 10 new words this week) versus presenting words in context. Presenting words in a line or column is advantageous in that it focuses students' attention on each word (Allred, 1984; Graham, 1983; Graham & Miller, 1979; Smith, 1975; Thomas, 1979). Moreover, presenting spelling words in lists can be complemented by giving the meanings of the words. For instance, many teachers who use the list method first pronounce the words out loud, read sentences

Table 5-2
Spelling Rules

1. Rules governing the addition of suffixes and inflected endings:

   a. When a word ends in "e", the "e" is usually dropped when a syllable beginning with a vowel is added.
   bake   baking
   make   making

   b. When a word ends in e the "e" is usually kept when a syllable beginning with a vowel is added.
   bake   baker
   make   maker

   c. When a root word ends in "y" and is preceded by a consonant, the "y" is changed to "i" when suffixes and endings are added unless they begin with an "i".
   fly   flies   fly   flying
   study   studies   study   studying

   d. When a noun ends in "y" and is preceded by a consonant, the plural is formed by changing the "y" to "i" and adding "es".
   baby   babies
   puppy   puppies

   e. When a root word ends in "y" and is preceded by a vowel, the root word is not changed when a suffix or ending is added.
   play   playful
   monkey   monkeys

   f. Words that end consonant and are preceded by a single vowel usually require that the consonant be doubled before adding an ending.
   run   running
   sit   sitting

2. Capital letters are used in the following situations:
   a. The first word of a sentence (He went home)
   b. The letter "I" when used as a word (Jimmy and I went fishing)
   c. Proper names (Tommy, Jane, Canada)
   d. Words derived from proper names (Canadian, French)
   e. Titles before proper names (Sir Winston Churchill)

Table 5-2 (cont.)
Spelling Rules

     f. The first and all important words of a book title, story, etc. (The Return of the Native)

3. Apostrophes are used in the following situations:
     a. An apostrophe and "s" to show possession after a single noun (the boy's coat)
     b. An apostrophe alone to show possession after a plural noun ending in "s" (the girls' coats)
     c. An apostrophe and "s" to show possession after a plural noun not ending in "s" (the children's coats)
     d. An apostrophe to show the omission of a letter or letters in a contraction (isn't, I'll)

4. Rules about the letter "s" and plurals.
     a. When adding "s" to words to form plurals or to change the tense of verbs; "es" must be added to words ending with hissing sounds. (x, s, sh, ch)
         glass   glasses
         watch watches
     b. When "s" is added to words ending in a single "f" to form plurals, the "f" is changed to "v" and "es" is added.
         wolf   wolves
         half   halves

5. Most abbreviations end with a period.
         Ont.
         Nov.

6. The letter "q" is always followed by "u" in common English words.
         queen
         quiet

7. No English words end in "v".
         glove
         move

8. The letter "i" usually comes before "e" except after "c".
         receive
         receipt

From Allred (1984), and Thomas (1979)

that include the words, and then read the words aloud again (Horn, 1967). Reading words in sentences presumably provides students with the opportunity to acquire the words' meanings via context. (See Chapter 4 for evidence that children do not acquire vocabulary meaning through context.)

Teach whole words. Spelling words are also better studied as whole words than in syllabified form (Allred, 1977; Allred, 1984; Graham, 1983). Students' attention should be focused on each word as a whole and not just the "hard-to-spell" spots. Visual attention directed to the whole word is presumed to aid in the formation of correct visual images which, in turn, enhance overall spelling retention.

Teach unknown words, not mixed lists. The study of unknown words only (i.e., test-study-test method, with only words misspelled on the first test retained for study) is superior to the study of both known and unknown words (i.e., study-test method; Allred, 1977; Allred, 1984; Fitzgerald, 1951b, 1953; Yee 1969; Graham & Miller, 1979). Prior to formal spelling instruction, a spelling test for potential target words is administered. The selection of spelling words should include those words that are frequently used by children in that grade so students will have meaningful opportunities to apply the words throughout the school year (see Thomas, 1979 for a review of the 3000 most common words used in elementary-grade children's writings). Words that are correctly spelled are not included in spelling instruction. If a spelling pretest is not administered, it is very likely that words currently part of students' spelling repertoires will be included in study. This, in turn, may lower students' motivation to acquire spelling skills. After study, students are again administered a spelling test. This spelling test should include both previously known and unknown words. The periodic testing of mastered words will help ensure spelling maintenance (Neef, Iwata, & Page, 1977). Misspelled words are then noted and incorporated into future lessons.

It is extremely important that teachers monitor and praise students' achievements. It has been recommended that students should monitor their own spelling progress (Wallace & Kauffman, 1978). For instance, students could record both the number of words correctly spelled at pretest, and the number of words spelled correctly at posttest. Self-monitoring can help provide students with motivation for learning spelling skills and help them gain a better sense of their spelling strengths and weaknesses and, at the same time, aid teachers in planning the course of future instruction (Graham, 1983; Thomas, 1979). Self-monitoring may be especially useful when working with children who do not have a clear sense of their own progress (i.e., learning disabled or mentally delayed children). In his book, Thomas (1979) provides examples of suitable record forms for students in elementary and senior grades.

Individualize spelling instruction. The importance and necessity of individualized spelling instruction cannot be overemphasized (e.g., Graham, 1983; Graham & Miller, 1979; Rowell, 1972). According to Graham (1983), individualized instruction implies that teachers be responsive to the unique needs of every student in their class, that teachers carefully choose materials that match the needs of individual students, and that the content of spelling programs be personalized. Furthermore, instruction should be planned, monitored, and modified on the basis of the individual student's performance. The teacher must assess the current strengths and weaknesses of every student, carefully monitoring both progress and changing needs. Spelling instruction should then be adapted to those needs.

We realize that with the large number of students in classrooms today (each of whom are uniquely different), the recommendation for individualized spelling instruction is not an easy one to carry out. Yet these suggestions can reduce the costs of personalized instruction. For example, by having students study only those words that they spell incorrectly at spelling pretest (i.e., the test-study-test method), teachers can ensure suitable study materials for each student without expending additional time testing any one student. (This is true because students are given the same spelling pretest and posttest but are instructed to study only those words they spelled incorrectly at pretest.) Similarly, by having students monitor their own spelling achievements, teachers can reduce their own record keeping, yet still have access to valuable information concerning each student. Individualized instruction does not imply that students need to work alone. Rather, it is recommended that students studying identical skills be instructed as a group (van Oudenhoven, Berkum, & Swen-Koopmans, 1987).

Use the microcomputer to improve spelling. The microcomputer promises to be a helpful aid in the delivery of individualized spelling instruction (Allred, 1984; Sears & Johnson, 1986). Not only can computers store and present large amounts of information, but children find using computers rewarding and fun. It is very probable that computers will soon be used to help provide individualized spelling drills and practice, diagnose spelling errors, and provide study direction (Allred, 1984).

Integrate spelling in written work. Finally, it must be remembered that correct spelling is not an end unto itself. Rather, spelling is an integral part of writing and should be taught in the context of general language study (Allred, 1984; Graham, 1983; Horn, 1967). It is important that students be given the opportunity to apply spelling skills they've learned to written work. A variety of instructional materials and approaches should be used. For instance, students can be asked to spell words in response to a picture or spell the word that completes a sentence. Children should be allowed to concentrate on personally required spellings (i.e., self-generated spellings) instead of copying words from a text. For example, students can be asked to develop spelling vocabularies that pertain to their special interests and hobbies (Thomas, 1979).

SPELLING ACQUISITION STRATEGIES

One very clear finding in the spelling literature is that children should not be left to their own devices to acquire effective spelling strategies (Allred, 1977; Allred, 1984; Gilstrap, 1962; Graham, 1983; Graham & Freeman, 1986; Graham & Miller, 1979). Teachers can help students acquire and maintain spelling competence by imparting effective spelling strategies that can be used to master both materials encountered in the spelling curriculum as well as those encountered outside of the classroom. According to Graham and Miller (1979), an effective spelling strategy leads to the acquisition of the whole word, requires careful pronunciation of the word, promotes visual imagery, provides auditory and/or kinesthetic reinforcement, and involves systematic testing of recall. Not surprisingly, there is no single best method for teaching spelling (Blair, 1975; Gerber & Lydiatt, 1984; Thomas, 1979). In the following section, empirically supported spelling techniques are out-lined and discussed. Ultimately, it is the teacher's decision which strategy or strategies should be taught. Depending upon the unique characteristics of the students in the classroom, it is very likely that certain strategies will be more appropriate for some students than for others.

Imagery Strategies [SSR]

Mental imagery facilitates various types of learning. For instance, Paivio and Yuille (1967) demonstrated that imagery instructions enhanced learn-ing of paired associates as long as the pair members were depicted in a common interaction. Similarly, research conducted within the last two decades has demonstrated that instructions to code sentence content imagi-nally enhance the retention of sentences (Anderson & Hidde, 1971; Pressley et al., 1987) and prose passages (Anderson & Kulhany, 1972; Rasco, Ten-nyson, & Boutwell, 1975). The use of imagery also improves acquisition of spelling skills (e.g., Sears & Johnson, 1986).

Radaker (1963) was among the first investigators to test whether mental imagery might aid children's acquisition of word spellings. Radaker trained 60 fourth-grade children to use an imagery strategy while studying spelling words. Radaker found that the children who were instructed to use mental imagery demonstrated superior spelling performances on subsequent spelling tests relative to children who were not instructed to use mental imagery.

When evaluated prior to imagery training (i.e., Stanford Achievement Test, Form M), the spelling scores of students instructed to use mental imagery did not differ from the scores of students who were not given imagery training. However, after training, students instructed to use mental imagery displayed superior spelling performance on a test of similar difficulty (i.e., Stanford Achievement Test, Form N). Only a few training sessions were required to teach the mental imagery study strategy adequately (i.e., performance scores were essentially equal whether students participated in two 45-minute imagery training sessions or six such sessions). Even more impressive, imagery-instructed children continued to demonstrate superior spelling achievements *one year* after training. Finally, Radaker's work confirmed the findings of other researchers who concluded that mental imagery was an effective study tool when learning to spell (e.g., Fitzgerald, 1951a; Gilstrap, 1962; Horn, 1919, cited in Graham & Miller, 1979) and suggested that instructions to use mental imagery can facilitate spelling performance over long periods of time.

The specific instructions used by Radaker are outlined in Table 5-3. Prior to imagery instruction, target words were selected that were unique in pattern, low in frequency, and relatively unfamiliar to the students. Students assigned to the imagery condition were instructed in groups of five and participated in either two or six training sessions, each of which lasted 45 minutes. Students assigned to the control condition were not directed to use any specific spelling study strategy other than the one they were

---

Table 5-3
Imagery training instructions

1. Select appropriate words for spelling instruction.

2. Imagery Training.
   a. Present words individually on flash-cards.
   b. Instruct students to read each word carefully, paying special attention to the word's letter sequence.
   c. Instruct students to close their eyes and imagine the word projected on a large outdoor screen in large, glossy black letters.
   d. Instruct students to hold their images in their minds for as long as possible.
   e. Instruct students who are experiencing difficulties stabilizing their images to imagine that they were nailing each letter of the word onto the theatre screen.
   f. Instruct students to imagine that they are pasting the letters of the word onto the theatre screen.
   g. Instruct students to image a floodlight illuminating the word letters so brightly that the letters will not fade until they dissolve their image of the word.

3. Instruct students to use the imagery technique whenever they were studying spelling words.

From Radaker (1963)

currently using and were assigned to six sessions of free play and social conversation.

In the first phase of imagery training, the children were presented with flash cards that displayed the printed target words. The flash cards were presented one at a time. The children were instructed to read each word carefully, paying special attention to the word's letter sequence. The children were then instructed to close their eyes and try to imagine the word being projected on a large outdoor screen. The word was to be imagined as printed in large, glossy black letters. When the children had created their mental image of the word, they were instructed to stabilize the image by holding it in their minds for as long as possible. The objective was to hold each image for one minute.

If students experienced difficulty stabilizing their images, they were instructed to imagine that they were nailing each letter of the word onto the theater screen. To help improve retention, all the students were instructed to imagine themselves applying paste to the back of the letters and gluing the words onto the screen. The children were instructed to nail and/or paste each letter of the word as it appeared sequentially. Students were also told to imagine that a floodlight was illuminating the words with such brightness that the words would not fade until the students dissolved their images. At the end of the training sessions, it was recommended that students use this imagery technique whenever they were studying spelling words.

To reiterate, Radaker found that children trained to use mental imagery spelled more words correctly on subsequent spelling tests relative to children who were not trained to use imagery, and that instructional gains were maintained at least one year following training. Further, only a brief instruction time was required to teach students the imagery strategy.

Although the instructions used by Radaker are appropriate for younger grade-school children, teachers may want to use alternative imagery instructions with older students. Tables 4 and 5 outline instructions used by Horn (1919, cited in Graham & Miller, 1979) and Fitzgerald (1951b). Essen-

---

Table 5-4
Imagery instructions

1. Look at the word and say it to yourself.
2. Close your eyes and visualize the word.
3. Check to see if you were right (if you were wrong, begin at step 1).
4. Cover the word and write it.
5. Check to see if you were right (if you were wrong, begin at step 1).
6. Repeat steps 4 and 5 two more times.

From Horn (1919), cited in Graham & Miller (1979)

Table 5-5
Imagery strategy

> 1. Look at the word carefully.
> 2. Say the word.
> 3. With your eyes closed, visualize the word.
> 4. Cover the word and then write it.
> 5. Check the spelling.
> 6. If the word is misspelled, repeat steps 1 to 5.

From Fitgerald (1951a)

tially, both Fitgerald and Horn instructed students to read spelling words carefully and then imagine the words in their minds. Without looking at the printed original, students were required to write the words down on paper. Each student then checked the accuracy of his or her spelling with the original. If any word was spelled incorrectly, the process was repeated (i.e., *look, visualize, cover, write, check*). Both older and younger students can be taught to use these imagery techniques when studying to-be-learned spelling items (e.g., Thomas, 1979). Older students in particular may prefer these later strategies to Radaker's "nail-and-paste" method.

Word Analogy Strategy [SSR]

The general rationale underlying the use of an analogy strategy is that the identification and use of known orthographic patterns will aid attempts to spell unknown words. Studies investigating the spelling skills of mature students have found that older students readily extract orthographic patterns of known words to spell unknown words (Hodges, 1982; Juola, Schadler, Chabot, & McCaughey, 1978). There is also evidence that by the second grade, some students spontaneously use familiar word patterns to help them spell unknown words (Beers, 1976; cited in Englert, Hiebert, & Stewart, 1985). Mildly handicapped students, however, appear to have difficulties spontaneously recognizing and using word patterns when attempting unknown spellings (e.g., Carpenter & Miller, 1982). Fortunately, with special training, these students can be taught to use analogy strategies successfully. For instance, Englert et al. (1985) found that when mildly handicapped children were taught to use analogy strategies, both the number of correct word spellings as well as the readability of misspellings were substantially improved. These authors advocate that spelling programs should include word classification activities and teach students to generate new words according to the orthographic patterns of known words.

Table 5-6
Analogy Strategy

1. Administer a pretest to select suitable target, practice, and transfer words for spelling instruction.
2. Have children learn and memorize the "Rhyming Rule".
   a. Tell the child that when two words rhyme, the last part of the words often are spelled the same.
   b. Provide examples of this rule.
   c. Have the child identify word from a word list that rhymes with an orally presented word.
   d. Have the child identify the letters that the two words share according to the Rhyming Rule.
3. Have children learn target rules via an imagery strategy.
   a. Child reads and spells out loud word.
   b. Child spells word out loud from memory (if word is spelled incorrectly, printed word is presented).
   c. Child writes word twice from memory (if word is spelled incorrectly, printed word is presented).
   d. Delayed spelling test is given.
4. Instruction and training using the analogy strategy.
   a. Child given word list that contains the studied target words.
   b. Child is required to pick target word that rhymes with an orally presented practice word.
   c. Child is required to identify the letters that the two words share.
   d. Child is encouraged to spell the practice word using the rhyming elements of the target word.
5. Expansion of analogy skills.
   a. The child is asked to complete cloze sentences using the practice words (children are allowed to look at their word list to help them do this).
   b. The child is asked to write the practice word without looking at their word list.
   c. If practice word is spelled incorrectly, a verbal prompt is given to think of words that rhyme with the practice word and how they are spelled.
   d. If verbal prompt is insufficient to produce correct spelling, the word list is given back to the child and they are asked to search for the target word that rhymes with the practice word.
   e. The procedure is reiterated until the practice word is spelled correctly.
6. Spelling test is given for target words and rhyming transfer words.

From Englert, Hiebert, & Stewart (1985)

Table 5-6 outlines the analogy instructions used by Englert et al. (1985). Twenty-two students participated in this study. Eighteen students were classified as learning disabled (verbal and performance WISC-R IQ = 90 or above) while the remaining four students were classified as educable mentally retarded (verbal and performance WISC-R IQ = 50-70). All the students lacked skills in reading and spelling. The only criterion for participation in the study was that students scored at least 80% on a rhyming pretest. Half the students were randomly assigned to an *imagery plus analogy training* condition while the other half were assigned to a control condition that entailed *imagery training* only.

Selecting the words for a pretest. Prior to training, 50 words were selected for acquisition. These core or target words were common words that rhymed and shared similar orthographic pattern with at least five other words. For each of the 50 target items, five rhyming and orthographically similar words were selected to be used as practice and transfer words. Thirty teachers were asked to review the sets of five rhyming words and choose from each set the one word that they considered to be the least common in the reading and spelling vocabularies of grade-2 children. These words became the noninstructed transfer words used to measure strategy generalization. The remaining four words from each set became the practice words used to teach the analogy strategy.

All the students were then administered a spelling pretest. The spelling abilities of the students assigned to the imagery plus analogy and imagery only training conditions did not differ significantly. Using the information acquired from the pretest, 15 misspelled target words and their respective practice and uncommon transfer words were selected for each student assigned to the imagery plus analogy training condition. Thirty misspelled target words were selected for each student assigned to the imagery only condition. Teachers held individual sessions with their students three times weekly, with sessions of approximately ten minutes apiece. The training program lasted four weeks.

To start the *imagery plus analogy* session, children were taught that *when two words rhyme, the last part of the words are often spelled the same.* Teachers provided demonstrations of this rule, and students were required to memorize and demonstrate an understanding of the rule. Instruction continued until students could accurately indicate which word from a list rhymed with an orally presented word, and could indicate which letters the two words shared according to the rhyming rule.

Teaching the imagery strategy. When the children had successfully demonstrated understanding of the rhyming rule, they were taught to use an *imagery strategy* to study the target spelling words (i.e., common words chosen from the spelling pretest). In this phase, the students were first asked to read and spell out loud three to four words. The children were then required to spell the words out loud from memory and write them twice without looking at the printed original. If a student misspelled a word, the child was again presented the printed version of the word and the procedure was repeated. Each student was given a delayed spelling test (at least one minute after the last word was presented) for all the target words. Training continued until each student could spell 15 words that he or she had been unable to spell at pretest.

Teaching the analogy strategy. During the third stage, students received instruction and training concerning *the use of the analogy strategy*. Students were asked to find items from a word sheet (the word sheet consisted of the target words learned via the imagery strategy) that rhymed with an orally presented practice word (i.e., rhyming words selected at pretest). The children were also asked to identify the letters in both words that were spelled the same. (This procedure is identical to that used in phase 1, where students were taught the rhyming rule.) Students were encouraged to spell the practice words using the rhyming elements of the target words.

In the final phase of training, students expanded their analogy skills. First, the children were asked to complete cloze sentences with the practice words. The children were allowed to consult their target word list to help them complete this task. Second, the children were asked to write the practice words without looking at their word list. If a practice word was spelled incorrectly, the student was prompted to think of words that rhymed with the practice word and how they were spelled. If the verbal prompt was insufficient to produce correct spelling, the student was shown his target word list and asked to search for the target word that rhymed with the problematic practice word. Once the student identified the appropriate target word, the procedure was repeated. Thus, the primary emphasis throughout the experimental sessions was to search for orthographic similarities between known and unknown words that rhymed, and to use shared letter patterns when spelling novel words.

Imagery only instructions. Students assigned to the *imagery only* condition were treated similarly with the exception that they were not given analogy training. In the first phase, children in this group were instructed to listen as the teacher read each of the 30 target words out loud. Next, they said the target words out loud in unison with their teacher, and finally, repeated the target words on their own.

In the second phase (i.e., the imagery training phase), the students were asked first to spell the target words out loud while looking at printed versions, and then to write the words from memory. If a word was misspelled, the printed word was shown to the student and the procedure was repeated. The procedure continued until the student wrote the target words successfully from memory twice and spelled the words correctly on a delayed test of recall.

Finally, students assigned to the imagery only condition practiced completing sentences with the target words and were encouraged to spell the words from memory. Again, if a word was spelled incorrectly, the list of the target words was presented to the student who was then required to copy the correct spelling of the word that completed the sentence.

The post training spelling test. A spelling test for both the selected target words (common words) and transfer words (uncommon words) concluded the training sessions. The number of correct spellings and the quality of errors committed by students given imagery plus analogy strategy training was compared to the spelling performances of students given imagery training only. Both groups improved in their ability to spell target words after training. This is not surprising considering that both groups were instructed to use an imagery strategy while studying the target words. By the end of the training session, students in the *imagery plus analogy training* group spelled significantly more transfer words correctly than did students in the imagery only group. Students instructed to use the *imagery plus analogy strategy* also demonstrated substantial improvement in the quality of spelling errors committed relative to students in the imagery only group. Specifically, at the time of pretest, 50% of the students in both groups were performing at the prephonetic spelling stage. The other 50% displayed errors characteristic of early transitional stage spelling. At posttest, however, only the students in the *imagery plus analogy* group showed advancement across the developmental stages. Over two-thirds of the *imagery plus analogy* students displayed either transitional stage errors or, even better, correct spellings.

Analogy training is an effective spelling strategy that can be used to help students generalize their knowledge of known orthographic patterns when spelling novel words. Without analogy training, control subjects improved their spellings of target words only; they did not transfer their newly acquired knowledge to orthographically similar words. Although Englert and her colleagues worked with mildly handicapped students, there is no apparent reason why their training program would not also benefit the spelling performances of poor spellers who do not spontaneously use analogy skills. Overall, the results support the authors' recommendation that educators teach students that when trying to spell an unknown word, it is sometimes helpful to think of the orthographic pattern of a known word. We also feel that analogy instruction is an effective and appropriate spelling strategy for the acquisition of words with common letter patterns, but that other strategies, such as imagery, are also required when words do not have this characteristic.

SPELLING CORRECTION STRATEGIES

Correct-Your-Own-Test Strategy [T]

The "correct-your-own-test" or "corrected-test" procedure has been acclaimed to be the *single* most effective strategy in teaching children to spell

(Graham & Miller, 1979; Thomas, 1979). When this strategy is used, students, under the supervision of their teachers, correct their own errors immediately after completing a spelling test (Kuhn & Schroeder, 1971; Allred, 1977; Hall, 1964; van Oudenhoven, Berkum, & Swen-Koopmans, 1987). Typically, the teacher will either spell the test words out loud as students correct their own work, or will write the proper spellings on the blackboard while students mark and correct any letter errors they may have committed (Kuhn & Schroeder, 1971; Hall, 1964). Older students may be instructed to check their work with words contained in a spelling textbook (Thomas, 1979).

The correct-your-own-test spelling procedure is probably among the first spelling strategies to be systematically researched and empirically tested. In 1946, Horn determined that self-correction procedures alone accounted for 90% to 95% of spelling gains that resulted from combined pronunciation exercises, self-test correction exercises, and study (cited in Graham & Miller, 1979; Hall, 1964; Thomas, 1979). Results of more recent research confirm that this method is an effective aid when learning spelling for both normal and learning disabled students (e.g., Allred, 1977; Hall, 1964; Kuhn & Schroeder, 1971; Stowitschek & Jobes, 1977).

Traditionally, use of the self-correction method requires students to correct their spellings as their teacher orally presents the correct spellings (e.g., Hall, 1964). Alternatively, there is evidence available suggesting that additional gains may be acquired if the correct spellings are presented in more than one sensory modality. For example, the teacher may use visual aids such as cue cards to point out the letters in the word while reading the correct spelling out loud (Stowitschek & Jobes, 1977). In such a situation, students can simultaneously see and listen to the proper word spellings while they correct their errors (Stowitschek & Jobes, 1977).

In one study investigating the spelling skills of 188 grade-4 and grade-6 students, Kuhn and Schroeder (1971) demonstrated that greater spelling gains were achieved when children were given combined visual and auditory feedback than when they were given auditory feedback only. Specifically, when students were provided with visual and auditory feedback, they displayed a consistent two-word spelling advantage relative to when they were just given auditory feedback. This was true for both students in the fourth and sixth grades, for both males and females, and for both high and low achievers (achievement was measured by the Iowa Tests of Basic Skills). The authors speculated that over an extended period of time, the number of words mastered by individuals provided with both visual and auditory feedback would be substantial.

The correct-your-own-test method is believed to facilitate spelling performance in a two-fold manner. First, the method presents the opportunity to discover which words are difficult to spell and, specifically, to locate the part(s) of those words that are particularly problematic. Second, the method demonstrates how to correct misspellings via the presentation of the correct spellings (Graham & Miller, 1979). Allowing students to monitor and correct their own spellings may also prove to be a motivating experience for students and provide them with an opportunity to self-diagnose their spelling progress (Thomas, 1979).

Occasionally, teachers will need to examine students' self-corrected tests. By examining the corrected work, teachers can check the accuracy of marking and supervise and assist those children who are having difficulties. Examination of a student's self-marked tests can also provide the teacher with information regarding the type of errors that the student is making. This information, in turn, may help the teacher decide upon the most appropriate course of future instruction. *Allowing students to monitor and correct their own spelling errors is a useful strategy that can be used in combination with other strategies. Whenever possible, the presentation of correct spellings should be in more than one sensory modality.*

Imitation Strategy [T]

Spelling performances of learning disabled and mentally delayed children have been improved when teachers imitated student's incorrect spellings in addition to providing the correct spellings (Gerber, 1984, 1986; Kauffman, Hallahan, Haas, Brame, & Boren, 1978). The training techniques used by Kauffman et al. (1978) are outlined in Table 5-7. The researchers instructed teachers to administer daily spelling instruction (i.e., phonic drills for phonetically regular words, drills with flash cards for irregular words, and practice writing all words on the chalkboard) and daily spelling tests for words that children spelled incorrectly at pretest. Teachers worked with the students on an individual basis for the first four days of the school week. Ten words consisting of five new words and five review words (excluding Monday where ten new words were given), were taught and tested each day. On Friday a spelling test was administered for all 20 words studied throughout the week.

Teachers were told to imitate and help students correct spelling errors during the daily testing of target words. If the student correctly spelled a word, they were immediately given praise. If, however, the student committed an error, the teacher both imitated the student's incorrect spelling and presented the correct spelling. Specifically, the teacher erased the student's spelling from the chalkboard (students wrote all words on the chalkboard), re-printed the student's incorrect spelling, and printed the correct spelling to the side. The teacher highlighted the incorrect letter(s) by boxing it. The child was then required to write the word correctly.

Kauffman et al. (1978) found that children who were shown both their incorrect spelling as well as the correct spelling, improved in their overall spelling skills. For example, one student demonstrated 92.5% spelling accuracy following error imitation plus correct spelling training relative to 82.5% spelling accuracy when he was shown the correct spelling only. The

---

Table 5-7
Error imitation plus self-correction training method

1. Daily instruction and testing for words spelled incorrectly at pretest.

2. Spelling tests were given immediately after instruction. The student was required to print his responses on the chalkboard.

3. If the student spelled the word correctly, praise was given.

4. If an error was made, the teacher said "No that's wrong" and erased the incorrect word.

5. The teacher then wrote the student's incorrect spelling on the board saying "Here's the way you spelled it".

6. The teacher wrote the correct spelling of the word beside the incorrect spelling and said "This is the way it is correctly spelled"

7. The teacher highlighted the incorrect letters by drawing a box around them.

8. The student was required to copy the correct spelling.

From Kauffman, Hallahan, Haas, Brame, & Boren (1978)

---

authors found that the positive effects of imitating students' errors in addition to showing them the correct spelling were more striking for phonetically irregular words than for phonetically regular words.

Gerber (1984; 1986) recently found additional evidence in favor of presenting students both incorrect and correct spellings. Like Kauffman et al. (1978), Gerber restricted his investigation to children who were either learning disabled or mentally delayed. Gerber found that children who were shown their misspellings in addition to the correct spellings, and who continually practiced spelling target items until they reached 100% spelling accuracy, displayed fewer spelling errors on a subsequent list of rhyming and structurally similar words. Not only did these children make fewer errors in their attempts to spell novel words (compared to their initial spelling performance for the target items), but the quality of their errors was markedly improved (i.e., students abandoned phonetic spellings for more plausible and conventional representations), and fewer trials were required to reach 100% spelling accuracy.

There are several reasons why the presentation of both incorrect and correct spellings should facilitate overall spelling performance. First, the presentation helps to focus the child's attention on how his spelling attempt differs from the correct spelling. (This rationale is identical to the principles underlying the correct-your-own-test technique.) In addition, Kauffman et al., argue that when phonetic rules do not apply to the spelling of unknown words, children must rely more heavily on visual memory. The visual presentation of the correct spelling probably improves the students' visual memory for the word, which in turn enhances spelling performance. Also, for most children five years of age and older, error imitation is an adverse situation, especially when accompanied by other actions that indicate that the behavior is inappropriate. Therefore, children will be more motivated to avoid such situations by producing correct spellings. Finally, like most forms of concept learning, spelling acquisition should be enhanced by the presentation of negative instances followed by positive instances (Kauffman et al., 1978).

Despite the apparent success of this strategy, we know of no investigations using the imitation method with non-disabled students. Although there is no theoretical reason why gains in spelling performance produced by this strategy should be limited to special education students, some degree of caution should be used prior to implementing this strategy in regular classrooms. It might be advisable to use this technique with a few students (to ensure that the method is suited for the needs of the particular children in the class), and then implement the technique on a larger scale. It is also possible that parents could be trained to administer the imitation and correction procedure with their children, alleviating some of the time teachers are required to spend with individual students.

Spelling Consciousness: Error Detection and Correction [T]

The ultimate purpose behind teaching children how to spell is that they generalize the knowledge and skill acquired during instructional periods to daily writing situations (Schell, 1975). Aside from teaching acquisition and correction strategies, another way we can help children spell accurately on a daily basis is to foster and promote strategies that allow them to know when a word is spelled either correctly or incorrectly, or to know when there is reason to be doubtful of a word's spelling (Valmont, 1972). Collectively, these skills are referred to as "spelling consciousness" and ideally occur during or after writing (i.e., proofreading).

As early as the 1920's, educators have acknowledged the importance of developing spelling consciousness (e.g., Pryor & Pittman; 1921 cited in Valmont, 1972). However, research conducted in the area was primarily concerned with assessing the amount of spelling consciousness subjects possessed. In general, persons of all ages lacked the ability to identify misspelled words, although the amount of spelling consciousness varied across different writing situations (Valmont, 1972).

Approximately twenty years ago, Personke and Lester (1967) developed a training program designed to facilitate proofreading skills. They empirically tested the effects of their program on spelling performance. Their project was based on the observation that the desire to spell correctly and the use of a dictionary were insufficient if individuals did not possess strategies for finding the spellings of unknown words.

The authors recruited 40 grade-6 children from two schools and randomly assigned them to either an experimental or control group. Prior to the training program, the children's IQ and spelling achievement scores (based on standardized tests given in the previous school year) were compared. There were no significant differences between the scores of children assigned to either the experimental or control groups. Throughout the course of the training sessions (fourteen lessons), students assigned to the experimental group practiced underlining words whose spellings were uncertain. Experimental students were also taught dictionary skills. The specific lesson plans used by the authors are listed in Table 5-8.

The training program was initiated by showing students in the experimental group a proofreading film and introducing the skills that would be taught in the lessons to follow. The children were instructed not to erase their spelling errors, but rather, to cross out any misspellings and write the correct spelling above the error. The next four lessons were devoted to improving dictionary skills and consisted of practicing alphabetical arrangements, using guidewords, and finding synonyms. For the sixth lesson, students were given a spelling chart containing common spellings of English sounds and were instructed how to use the chart when spelling difficult words. The chart was an enlargement from a page of a dictionary similar to the one displayed in Table 5-9. The children practiced using the chart by looking for errors inserted into a prepared manuscript. For the remaining lessons, the students wrote and proofread dictated passages as well as their own compositions. Before papers were collected, students were given time to proofread their work and were encouraged to make use of the sound spelling charts when seeking correct spellings. The program terminated with children writing and proofreading a letter that was mailed to a friend.

Children assigned to the control group were provided with equal writing opportunity and dictionary practice. Students in the control group, however, were not instructed how to use the common sounds spelling chart or told about the importance of proofreading. The stories were then used to assess the frequency of spelling errors between the two groups.

The percentage of spelling errors was computed for each paper by dividing the number of spelling errors by the total   number of running words. Children in the experimental group made significantly fewer spelling errors than did children in the control group. Even though the experimental group had less writing time than did the control group (due to time allotted for proofreading), the number of running words did not differ between the groups. Although some caution must be used when interpreting these results (i.e., the pre-training and post-training spelling measures were not equated for difficulty; there was no measure of vocabulary level or the number of different words written), the study suggests that using a dictionary alone is not sufficient to enhance proofreading for spelling errors.

Table 5-8
Lesson plans for proofreading training program

Lesson 1   Presentation of proofreading film and introduction to techniques to be used in subsequent lessons.

Lesson 2   Development of dictionary skills via practice in alphabetical arrangements, use of guidewords, and finding synonyms.

Lesson 3   Same as Lesson 2.

Lesson 4   Same as Lesson 2.

Lesson 5   Same as Lesson 2.

Lesson 6   Introduction in how to use the common sounds spelling chart when looking for the spelling of unknown words. Specifically, use the chart by taking the first best sound alternative. If this does not work, use the second best sound alternative and so on.

Lesson 7   Practice looking for errors in a prepared manuscript which contained errors designed to give children practice using the sounds spelling chart.

Lesson 8   Practice writing and proofreading a dictated paragraph.

Lesson 9   Practice writing and proofreading a personal composition, in this case a book report.

Lesson 10   Practice writing and proofreading a dictated paragraph containing difficult spelling words.

Lesson 11   Practice proofreading lists of spelling words selected as being particularly difficult for elementary school children. Words selected also provided the opportunity for children to use either the first or second sound choice according to their spelling charts.

Lesson 12   Same as Lesson 11.

Lesson 13   Practice proofreading a personal composition of a summary of a story read in their basal readers.

Lesson 14   Practice writing and proofreading a letter that will be mailed to a friend.

From Personke & Lester (1967)

Instead, children need to be explicitly told about the importance of proofreading and given strategic instruction concerning how to use the dictionary when finding words with unknown spellings. The authors conclude with the recommendation that proofreading instruction be included as part of the regular spelling curriculum.

Although the Personke and Lesters (1967) study represents one of the few empirical investigations addressing the development of spelling con-

Table 5-9
Spelling Sound Chart

KEY TO PRONUNCIATION

as in făte, āle, ā'corn, be-rāte', nat"u-ral-i-zā'tion.
" " fär, fä'ther, ärch, mär'shal, cär-toon'; also as in whät, wänt.
" " fȧst, glȧss, a-lȧs'; also as in so'dȧ, ȧ-dapt'ȧ-ble.
" " fạll, pạw, ạw'ful, ap-plạud'.
" " fĭ'nȧl, sea'mȧn, tol'er-ȧnt, men'ȧce.
" " cãre, ãir, mil'i-tãr-y, de-clãre'.
" " at, ac-cord', com-par'i-son, car'ry.

" " ēve, mēte, hē, Ē'den, in-ter-vēne'; also as in hēre, drēar'y.
" " prẹy, ẹight, o-bẹy'.
" " hẽr, vẽrse, sẽr'vice, in-tẽr'.
" " met, ebb, en-dorse', mon'e-tar-y, dis-tend'.
" " feed, pro-ceed', lee'way.

" " pīne, ī-de'a, īce'berg, de-cīde', al-lī'ance.
" " clĭque, ma-rĭne'; also as in Mar-tī'ni.
" " bĭrd, stĭr, ex'tĭr-pate, fĭrm'a-ment.
" " it, hit, re-mit', cit'y; also as in pos'si-ble, grav'i-ty, pu'pil.

" " nōte, ōat, sō, ō'pen, hel-lō'; also as in ren'ō-vate, prō-pel'.
" " mŏve, prŏve, tŏmb.
" " lọng, crọss, ọff, ọrb, fọr-bid', dọr'mer.
" " at'ŏm, plŏv'er; also as in ac'tŏr, wŏrd, wŏrk.
" " not, for'est, non'sense; also as in dog, broth, cost; also as in con-fess', con-cur'.
" " mọọn, cọọ, fọọd, brọọd'er.
" " book, hood, foot, look, cook'y.

" " ūse, fūse, ū-til'i-ty, fū'tile, im-mūne'.
" " bụll, pụt, fụl-fil', boun'ti-fụl.
" " brüte, jü'ry; also used for the German ü.
" " tûrn, fûr, bûr-lesque', de-mûr'.
" " up, rub, sun'set, in-sult'.

" " crȳ, eȳe.
" " myth, cit'y.

" " çat, to-baç'ço.
" " ma-chine'.
" " ace, ce'dar.
" " church.
" " chord.

ġ   as in ġem.
ñ   " " añ'ger, sphiñx.
ṅ   " " French boṅ.
ng   " " ring.
ş   " " mi'şer, aş.

th   " " this.
th   " " thin.
ẕ   " " aẕure.

au   " " umlaut.
aw   " " straw.

ou   " " out.
oi   " " oil.
oy   " " boy.

ew   " " new, few.

ow   " " now.

-tûre   as -chẽr (in picture).
-tion   } as -shun (in nation, tension).
-sion   }

-ciȧn   } as -shun (in Martian, Melanesian, mortician).
-tiȧn   }
-siȧn   }

-şiȧn   } as -zhun (in Persian, fusion).
-şion   }

-liŏn   as -lyun or -yun (in million).

-ceous   } as -shus (in cretaceous, delicious, conscious).
-(s)cious }

qu   as kw (in queen).
-ous   as -us (in porous).

ph-   as f- (in phone, etc.).

-le   as -l (at end of syllable, as in able, cycle, etc.).

-iȧ   as -yȧ (in pharmacopoeia).

wh-   as hw- in whale, etc.

kh   as in German doch (dokh).

Table 5-10
Summary of proofreading recommendations and suggestions

1. Ensure that initial spelling instruction is of a high quality; use empirically validated organization, acquisition, and correction spelling strategies. The quality of initial spelling instruction is believed to effect children's later abilities to proofread.

2. Stress the importance of accurate spelling and proofreading in both formal and social communications.

3. Provide adequate time for students to proofread, correct, and copy assignments before they are collected.

4. Have Students "tag" potential spelling errors. Students can tag words that they think are spelled wrong by underlining or circling them. The process of confirming uncertain spellings will strengthen recognition for correctly spelled words and provide feedback regarding misspelled words. Help children find spelling errors that are not tagged by placing a mark on the line the error occurs.

5. Familiarize children with the structure of dictionaries (i.e., alphabetical orderings and the use of guide words) and instruct children on how to use the dictionary when looking for an unfamiliar word's spelling. For example, instruct students to listen to the beginning sound of the word in question and try to locate the word based on this sound. If this fails, try to think of other letters that represent the sound.

6. Help students create and use other resources. For instance, creating a personal dictionary with index cards, using a class list of frequently misspelled words, or asking a friend to edit an assignment.

7. Help maintain students' interests with the occasional use of proofreading games. For suggestions see Graham, Freeman, and Miller (1981) and Hodges (1982).

8. Have children use computer software packages when editing written work. See Devant (1984) for comments on suitable computer packages.

From Bamburg (1977), Barnard Kendrick (1980), Lydiatt (1984), and Schell (1975) sciousness, many untested recommendations and suggestions have been proposed. Because it is important to promote spelling consciousness, we have listed some of these suggestions in Table 5-10, including ensuring high quality spelling instruction, providing adequate time for proofreading and correcting activities, promoting strategic approaches when finding unfamiliar spellings in a dictionary, and encouraging the use of other spelling resources. It should be remembered that the following are only suggestions and that their impact on spelling consciousness have not been systematically evaluated yet. Therefore, caution should be used prior to implementing any of these in the classroom. We suggest that teachers test the suitability of the activity in question with a small number of students prior to involving the whole class.

Concluding Comments

Although spelling has been studied extensively, there is currently nationwide concern that primary school students are not being taught the basics of spelling. It is a well known fact that many school-aged children experience difficulties spelling, especially students who are learning disabled or mentally delayed. It is likely that less than adequate teaching materials and instructional methods increase students' difficulties. Unfortunately, empirically validated instructional techniques are often neglected in favor of more traditional teaching methods (Graham, 1983). Changes can occur in the spelling curriculum if teachers are made aware of spelling strategies that really work. Those techniques were reviewed here. The gap between spelling research and classroom instruction can be narrowed. Teachers can include well validated strategies into their classrooms; researchers can extend their efforts to inform teachers about new findings. In addition to chapters like this one, there are other materials available to help bridge the gap between teaching and research. One of the best of these is a journal, *Spelling Progress Quarterly*. Both teachers and researchers can benefit from reading and contributing to such resources.

REFERENCES

Allred, R. (1977). *Spelling: The application of research findings.* Washington. D.C. National Education Association.

Allred, R. (1984). *What research says to the teacher: Spelling, trends, content, and methods.* Washington, D.C.: National Education Association.

Anderson, R.C., & Hidde, J.L. (1971) Imagery and sentence learning. *Journal of Educational Psychology, 63,* 242-243.

Anderson, R.C., & Kulhavy, R.W. (1972). Imagery and prose learning. *Journal of Educational Psychology, 63,* 242-243.

Bamberg, B. (1977) *Putting correctness in its place.* Study prepared at the University of Southern California. 12 P. Available ERIC *ED 162 340.*

Barnard, D.P., & Kendrick, R. (1980). If you want to improve student spelling. *The Clearing House, 54,* 164-167.

Beers, J.W., & Henderson, E.H. (1977). A study of developing orthographic concepts among first graders. *Research in the Teaching of English,* 11, 133-148.

Blair, T. (1975) ERIC/RCS. *Reading Teacher, 28,* 604-607.

Blake, H., & Emans, R. (1970). Some spelling facts. *Elementary English, 47,* 242-249.

Block, J. (1972). But will they ever lern to spel korectly? *Educational Research,* 14, 171-178.

Burbe, W. (Ed.) *Spelling Progress Quarterly.*

Carpenter, D. & Miller, L. (1982) Spelling ability of reading disabled LD students and able readers. *Learning Disability Quarterly, 5,* 65-70.

Cramer, R. (1969) The influence of phonic instruction on spelling achievement. *The Reading Teacher, 22,* 499-503.

Cronnell, B., & Humes, A. (1980). Elementary spelling: What's really taught. *The Elementary School Journal, 81,* 59-64.

Devail, T. (1984) Using the computer to strengthen spelling. *The Computing Teacher, 19,* 19-21.

Downing, J., DeStefano, J., Rich, G., & Bell, A., (1985). Children's views of spelling. *The Elementary School Journal, 85,* 185-198.

Drake, D., & Ehri, L. (1984). Spelling acquisition: Effects of pronouncing words on memory for their spellings. *Cognition and Instruction, 1,* 297-320.

Englert, C., Hiebert, E., & Stewart, S. (1985) Spelling unfamiliar words by an analogy strategy. *The Journal of Special Education, 19,* 291-306.

Fitgerald, J. (1951a) *A basic life spelling vocabulary.* Milwaukee: Bruce Publishing Co.

Fitgerald, J. (195lb). Methods of teaching spelling. *The teaching of spelling.* Milwaukee: Bruce Publishing Co.

Fitgerald, J. (1953) The teaching of spelling. *Elementary English, 30,* 79-84.

Fitzsimmons, R., & Loomer, B. (1977). *Spelling research and practice.* Iowa City: Iowa State Department of Public Instruction and The University of Iowa.

Gerber, M. (1984) Techniques to teach generalizable spelling skills. *Academic Therapy, 20,* 49-58.

Gerber, M. (1986) Generalization of spelling strategies by LD students as a result of contingent imitation/modeling and mastery criteria. *Journal of Learning Disabilities, 19,* 530-537

Gerber, M., & Lydiatt, S. (1984). Research and practice in teaching spelling. *Academic Therapy, 20,* 5-10.

Gillingham, A., & Stillman, B. (1969) *Remedial training for children with specific disability in reading, spelling and penmanship.* Cambridge, Mass.: Educators Publishing Service.

Gilstrap, R. (1962). Development of independent spelling skills in the intermediate grades. *Elementary English, 39,* 481-483.

Graham, S. (1983) Effective spelling instruction. *Elementary School Journal, 83,* 560-568.

Graham, S. & Freeman, S. (1986). Strategy training and teacher -vs- student-controlled study conditions: Effects on LD students' spelling performance. *Learning Disability Quarterly, 9,* 15-22.

Graham, S., Freeman, S., & Miller, L. (1981). *Spelling Games and Activities.* Department of Education, Washington, D.C. Available ERIC *ED 208 425.*

Graham, S., & Miller, L. (1979) Spelling research and practice: A unified approach. *Focus on Exceptional Children, 12,* 1-16.

Hahn, W. (1964). Phonics: A boon to spelling. *Elementary School Journal, 64,* 148-157.

Hall, N. (1964). The letter mark-out corrected test. *The Journal of Educational Research, 58,* 148-157.

Hall, R. (1984). Orthographic problem-solving. *Academic Therapy, 20,* 67-75.

Hanna, P., Hanna, J., Hodges, R., & Rudorf, E. (1967). Linguistic cues for spelling improvement. *Elementary English, 44,* 862-865.

Henderson, E.H., & Beers, J.W. (1980). Developmental strategies of spelling competence in primary school children. *Developmental and cognitive aspects in learning to spell: A reflection of word knowledge.* Newark, DE: International Reading Association.

Hildreth, G. (1956). Beginnings of spelling. *Teaching spelling: Guide to basic principles and practices.* New York: Holt & Company, Inc.

Hillerich, R., (1982). That's teaching spelling??? *Educational Leadership, 39,* 615-617.

Hodges, R.E. (1982). *Improving spelling and vocabulary in the secondary school. Theory and research into practice (TRIP)* Urbana, IL. National Council of Teachers of English. Available ERIC. *ED 218 645.*

Horn, E. (1926). *A basic vocabulary: 10,000 words most commonly used in writing.* Iowa City: University of Iowa.

Horn, E. (1967) *Teaching spelling: What research says to the teacher.* Washington DC. American Educational Research Association.

Horn, T. (1969) Research critiques. *Elementary English, 46,* 210-212.

Horn, T., & Otto, H. (1954) *Spelling instruction: A curriculum-wide approach.* Austin: University of Texas.

Ibeling, K. (1961) Supplementary phonics instruction and reading and spelling ability. *Elementary School Journal, 63,* 152-156.

Juola, F., Schadler, M., Chabot, R. & McCaughey, M. (1978). Development of visual processing skills related to reading. *Journal of Experimental Child Psychology, 25*, 230-240.

Kauffman, J., Hallahan, D., Haas, K., Brame, T., & Boren, R. (1978) Imitating children's errors to improve their spelling performance. *Journal of Learning Disabilities, 11*, 33-38.

Kuhn, J., & Schroeder, H. (1971). A multi-sensory approach for teaching spelling. *Elementary English, 48*, 863-869.

Lydiatt, S. (1984) Error detection and correction in spelling. *Academic Therapy, 20*, 33-40.

Marino, J. (1980) What makes a good speller? *Language Arts, 57*,173-177.

Mcllroy, K. (1976) *Helping the poor speller.* Auckland: Heinemann Educational Books.

Neef, N., Iwata, B., & Page, T. (1977) The effects of known item interspersal on acquisition and retention of spelling and sight word reading. *Journal of Applied Behavior Analysis, 10*, 738.

Paivio, A., & Yuille, J.C. (1967). Mediation instructions and word attributes in paired-associate learning. *Psychonomic Science, 8*, 65-66.

Personke, C., & Lester, K. (1967). Proofreading and spelling: A report and a program. *Elementary English, 44*, 768-774.

Personke, C., & Tee, A. (1971) *Comprehensive spelling instruction: Theory, research, and application.* Scranton: Intext Educational Publishers. Available ERIC *ED 052 204.*

Pressley, M., McDaniel, M.A., Turnure, J.E., Wood, E., & Ahmad, M. (1987) Generation and precision of elaboration: Effects on intentional and incidental learning. *Journal of Experimental Psychology: Learning, Memory, and Cognition, 13*, 291-300.

Radaker, L. (1963) The effect of visual imagery upon spelling performance. *The Journal of Educational Research, 56*, 370-372.

Radebaugh, M. (1985) Children's perceptions of their spelling strategies. *The Reading Teacher, 38*, 532-536.

Rasco, R.W., Tennyson, R.D., & Boutwell, R.C. (1975) Imagery instructions and drawings in learning prose. *Journal of Educational Psychology, 67*, 188-192.

Reith, H., Axelrod, S., Anderson, R., Hathaway, F, Wood, K., & Fitzgerald, C. (1974) Influence of distributed practice and daily testing on weekly spelling tests. *Journal of Educational Research, 68,* 73-77.

Rinsland, H. (1945) *A basic vocabulary of elementary school children.* New York: Macmillan Co.

Rowell, G. (1972) A prototype for an individualized spelling program. *Elementary English, 49,* 335-340.

Sears, N., & Johnson, D. (1986) The effects of visual imagery on spelling performance and retention among elementary students. *Journal of Educational Research, 79,* 230-233.

Schell, L. (1975) B+ in composition: C- in spelling. *Elementary English, 52,* 239-257.

Schoephoerster, H. (1962). Research into variations of the test study plan of teaching spelling. *Elementary English, 39,* 460-462.

Smith, H. (1975) Teaching spelling. *British Journal Educational Psychology, 45,* 68-72.

Stowitschek, C., & Jobes, N. (1977). Getting the bugs out of spelling: Or an alternative to the spelling bee. *Teaching Exceptional Children, 9,* 74-76.

Templeton, S. (1983) Using the spelling/meaning connection to develop word knowledge in older students. *Journal of Reading,* 8-14.

Thomas, V. (1972). The basic writing vocabulary of elementary school children. *The Alberta Journal of Educational Research, 18,* 243-248.

Thomas, V. (1979). *Teaching spelling: Canadian word lists and instructional techniques. Second Edition.* Gage Publishing Limited.

Valmont, W. (1972). Spelling consciousness: A long neglected area. *Elementary English, 49,* 1219-1265.

van Oudenhoven, J., Berkum, G., Swen-Koopmans, T. (1987) Effect of cooperation and shared feedback on spelling achievement. *Journal of Educational Psychology, 79,* 92-94.

Wallace, G., & Kauffman, J. (1978) *Teaching Children with Learning Problems.* Columbus, Ohio: Charles E. Merrill Publishing Company.

Webster's New Universal Unabridged Dictionary, Deluxe Second Edition. (1983) New York: New World Dictioanries/Simon and Schuster

Weisberg, P. (1985). *Teaching Spelling to the Learning Disabled in Traditional and Remedial Approaches: A Workshop*. Paper presented at the International Conference of the Association for Children and Adults with Learning Disabilities, San Francisco, CA. Available ERIC. ED *256 118*.

Yee, A. (1969) Is the phonetic generalization hypothesis in spelling valid? *Journal of Experimental Education, 37*, 82-91.

Zutell, J. (1979) Spelling strategies of primary school children and their relationship to Piaget's concept of decentration. *Research in the Teaching of English, 13*, 69-80.

CHAPTER 6

Writing

Researchers have shown an increased interest in writing instruction over the last decade (Hillocks, 1984). Before that, children were expected to learn how to write following instruction in the mechanics of writing (e.g., spelling, punctuation, and sentence format) with little, if any, attention given to higher-order writing strategies. It was assumed that students learned to write from reading and analyzing published texts and noting their structure and organizational features. The learner's role was to discover what was expected, with little guidance from the teacher. The process-oriented approach to writing provides a new role for teachers—to convey to children how to construct coherent text (Applebee, 1982; Dominic, 1983). The student uses the strategies that are taught, recognizing that the first draft is not the finished product and that teachers and peers can provide feedback as to how to improve the document.

There are a variety of strategic-process models, all premised on the belief that there are particular processes that can be carried out to produce coherent compositions. These include brainstorming, focusing on ideas and experiences of the writer, recruiting feedback from readers with diverse perspectives, revising, postponement of attention to editing, spelling, and grammar until the final draft, and the elimination or deferment of evaluation until the composition is complete (Applebee, 1981).

One of the earliest models of writing was presented by Rohman (1965), who portrayed writing as involving three stages: pre-writing (i.e., planning), writing (i.e., composing the draft), and rewriting (i.e., editing and revising). This theory was criticized in the 1970s because it was a linear model that failed to incorporate the recursive nature of the writing process. That is, writing does not occur in a strict plan, write, and rewrite order. Rather, planning occurs both before and during writing and bits and pieces are rewritten before a finished draft is constructed (Hayes & Flower, 1986).

Flower and Hayes (1980) have been credited with the identification of the recursive writing process. Many of the techniques of writing instruction are based on their theory. According to this model there are three units involved in mature writing: the writer's long-term memory, the environment of the writer, and writing itself, which can be further broken down into three processes: planning, translating, and reviewing.

Planning involves three sub-processes: a) generating— the retrieval of items from memory; b) organizing—the selection of the most useful of the materials retrieved by generating; and c) goal-setting—the judging of materials retrieved by generating as to whether they serve the current purpose of writing.

Translating involves taking material from memory under the guidance of a writing plan and transforming it into acceptable written English sentences.

Reviewing involves improving the quality of the written material using two sub-processes: a) reading (i.e. reading the segment of the text being reviewed); and b) editing—the detection and correction of violations in writing conventions and of inaccuracies of meaning, and the evaluation of materials with respect to the writing goals.

It should be noted that although these three processes are listed in a specific order, they do not necessarily occur in this sequence. Because this is a recursive model, processes and subprocesses may be executed in any order (e.g., one may backtrack from translating to planning; review can occur before anything has been written on paper). [See Table 6-1 for an example of planning, translating, and reviewing.]

One of the biggest problems that writing researchers have faced is trying to understand why some children who have a command of the language are such poor writers. The answer may be that writing and speaking are separate, distinct processes. For example, writers do not have the audience that they would if they were speaking. When a person is speaking to an audience they receive feedback such as head nods to continue, or quizzical looks and questions that suggest a need for clarification. In writing, however, the writer must anticipate the questions of the reader and answer any questions that may arise (McCutchen & Perfetti, 1983; Scardamalia & Bereiter, 1985). In addition, many times the motivation to learn how to write coherent prose is low due to the evaluation criteria used in schools. For instance, Odell (1980) believes that students are implicitly taught that writing is not important since competence in school is often documented by performance on multiple-choice and short-answer questions. When writing is taught, there seems to be undue concern about the lower-level mechanics of writing such as spelling and punctuation (e.g., Scardamalia, 1981), rather than on higher-order organizational skills.

In order to decide how writing instruction should be changed, it is necessary to understand how the quality of writing varies with instruction. In a descriptive study of 10 classrooms, Perl (1983) found that writing is better in classrooms where writing is taken more seriously. The nature of writing is often viewed as social in these classes, in that children can share their writing with the class (a less critical audience than the teacher or mom and dad) or children can collaborate on a piece of writing. There are connections made between reading, writing, and literature, with these literacy skills taught as interrelated. There is negotiation between the teacher and the student, including control over the written product. Finally, good writing teachers reflect on the instructional methods that are used in the classroom. That classrooms can be identified where writing is better than in others suggests that differences in teaching might be engineered that can

Table 6-1
Processes of Writing

Question: What did you do on your summer vacation?
"OK, let's see. I have to write about my summer vacation. What do I want to say. I went to the beach with my parents for a week. *(planning)* Actually, I went to the cottage is probably a better thing to say. *(reviewing)* When we were at the cottage we had a big bonfire down by the lake with some of the other cottages. I also went to a day camp and played games and made crafts. *(planning)* Yes now I've planned what I want to say and I can write."

Written Text:
During my summer vacation I went to the cottage with my family. We did alot of exciting things. My favorite was the big bonfire at the lake with all the other cottages. For the rest of the summer I went to a day camp where we did crafts and played games. I had a fun summer. *(translating)*

"OK, let's see what I have. Oops, I've made some mistakes, better fix those up. A lot is two words and did crafts should be made crafts. Maybe I should write a little more about the cottage. *(reviewing)* What else did I do? Oh yeah, we went swimming and at the bonfire we roasted hot dogs and marshmallows, plus we got to stay up late, that's why it was my favorite thing. What about the new friend that I made at camp. Yeah, I should talk about Jenny. *(planning)* All right, uhm, maybe I won't include just the swimming at the cottage, I should add a few more things and then say that the fire was my favorite. *(reviewing and planning)* We also went into town and had pizza one night and then there were the daily trips to the store for ice cream. *(planning)* OK, I'm ready to write again."

Revised Text:
During my summer vacation I did some interesting things. At the beginning of the summer I went to the cottage with my family for one week. While we were there we did a lot of exciting things like swimming, going for pizza, getting ice cream and having a bonfire. I liked having the bonfire the best because we roasted wieners and marshmallows and we got to stay up really late.
      During the rest of the summer I went to a day camp. We played a lot of fun games and made crafts. I met a girl named Jenny. She just moved into the neighborhood and is now going to my school. My summer was special because I made a new friend. *(translating)*

"Yes, I think that is exactly what I want to say."

From Flower & Hayes (1980)

produce improved writing.

Much of the writing improvement research has been conducted with poor child writers. There was an assumption for some time that average and above average child writers function well enough to get by without strategy instruction. In contrast, poor writers were assumed not to learn strategies on their own and, therefore, needed to be taught them. Nonetheless, it has become apparent in recent research that children generally are not highly proficient writers and even those who are writing at an above average level for their age still have a lot to learn (Scardamalia & Bereiter, 1985). Thus, the new strategy instruction is designed for a broad range of writing abilities.

Cognitive Strategy Instruction in Writing [T & SSR]

Englert and Raphael (1988) have developed a program which focuses on teaching writing strategies to fourth and fifth grade students through verbal modeling. This program is based on three different approaches to writing instruction developed over the past few years.

The first of these approaches is a process-writing approach that focuses on motivation and includes 1) daily writing on topics selected by the students, 2) peer evaluations through group presentations and editing, 3) publication of student papers, and 4) writing conferences (Bos, 1988; Graves, 1983). Students' motivation to write increases since they are able to choose topics which are of particular interest to them. The major criticism of this approach, when presented in isolation, is that children are left on their own to learn how to write without teacher intervention.

Englert and Raphael (1988) amalgamated these motivational features with two other instructional models that attend more explicitly to the "hows" of writing. *Schema-building* involves providing students with information on text structure so they may build up the knowledge of what is required when writing (e.g., a narrative story).

Fitzgerald and Teasley (1986) have found that teaching fourth grade children the structure of narrative stories increases their ability to write organized and coherent stories. Simply providing the children with an organization for text does not necessarily mean that students will understand the structure can be used to improve writing. They refer to the resulting composite intervention as Cognitive Strategy Instructing in Writing (CSIW). CSIW includes a lot of explanatory monologues. When teachers use think-alouds (verbal modeling) when writing (i.e., they make their thought processes transparent as they write), the children are provided an opportunity to observe the processes that guide a good writer.

CSIW incorporates all of these features into one large program of writing instruction that can be taught in the classroom (See Table 6-2). The first step in the program is to introduce children to text structure and strategies through the use of various examples. These examples range from poorly

Table 6-2
Cognitive Strategy Instruction in Writing (CSIW)

Step 1
Introduce children to text structure and strategies through the use of various examples.

Step 2
Introduce the plan think sheet.

Step 3
Introduce the organization think sheet.

Step 4
Have children create the first draft.

Step 5
Introduce the edit think sheet.

Step 6
Introduce the editor think sheet and have the children evaluate each other's papers.

Step 7
Introduce the revise think sheet and have the children revise their writing.

structured text to ones that are well structured. While reading a passage aloud, the teacher verbalizes questions about the passage. These are questions that might not be clear from reading alone (e.g., "I wonder how the author got into this situation?"). In generating these questions and overtly grappling with them, the teacher makes clear that it is not possible to know what is happening unless the information is written as part of the story.

Teachers then introduce "think-sheets" that guide students through the process of writing. These "think-sheets" provide an external copy of questions that should be posed as part of writing. The external availability of questions presumably frees some cognitive capacity that might otherwise be used to try and remember the questions. The plan think-sheet (See Figure 6-1) *allows the children to think of their audience* ("Who am I writing for?"; "Why am I writing this?"), *activate their background knowledge* ("What do I know about this topic?"), *and organize their ideas prior to and during the writing process* ("How can I group my ideas?"). The organization think-sheet (See

Figure 6-1
Plan "think-sheet"

Name _____   Date _____

Topic _____

WHO: Who am I writing for?

_____

_____

WHY: Why am I writing this?

_____

_____

_____

_____

WHAT: What do I know? (Brainstorm)

1. _____

2. _____

3. _____

4. _____

5. _____

6. _____

7. _____

8. _____

HOW: How can I group my ideas?

How will I organize my ideas?

__Comparison/Contrast   __Problem/Solution
__Explanation   __Other

Figure 6-2) allows children to focus on text structure with questions such as "What is being explained?" and "In what order do things happen?"

Once children have used these sheets to create their first draft, they are asked to edit their own text critically. At this point another think-sheet is introduced. The edit think-sheet (See Figure 6-3) allows students to focus on both the content and the organization of the paper. Since the check for organization section (i.e., Question Yourself) can be related back to the organization think-sheet, students are able to monitor their progress. The next step involves peer evaluation with the editor think-sheet (See Figure 6-4). This process is the same as the editing process except that it is now done by a peer instead of the person who wrote the text. In the final step the children review the editorial comments and revise as necessary (see Figure 5). Children's memory of these processes is facilitated with the acronym "P.O.W.E.R." (i.e., Plan, Organize, Write, Edit, Revise) (Stevens & Fear, 1987). Acronyms can be useful in reducing the dependency on "think-sheets" once students understand how to plan, organize, edit, and revise.

The research and analyses on CSIW are ongoing, but the preliminary results are positive. In a teacher-oriented study Raphael, Englert and Anderson (1987) interviewed two teachers who had been deemed "more successful" and "less successful" in implementing the CSIW. They found that children participated equally in the two classrooms, but that there were differences in the lesson content and the lesson segmentation. The "more successful" teacher used the opportunities to evaluate the students' knowledge base, modelled strategy use and, to a lesser degree, corrected misconceptions. The "less successful" teacher made less use of opportunities to evaluate students' progress and often introduced misconceptions of the goals of writing. The "less successful" teacher appeared to equate editing with writing and focused on the idea of impressing the audience rather than communicating ideas. In an extension of this research, Anthony, Gregg, and Englert (1987) found that students of more successful teachers were better able to write informational text than the students of teachers who were less successful in implementing CSIW.

Other preliminary analyses suggest clear qualitative differences in the structures of the essays written by CSIW-trained students (Englert & Raphael, in press; Stevens, Anthony, & Englert, 1988). Specifically, the CSIW essays incorporate the elements covered on the "think-sheets" and do so in more coherent ways than do non-trained controls. CSIW covers important information about writing and seems to promote children's knowledge and use of strategies for writing. Students' awareness that they can become efficient writers also increases.

Self-Control Strategy Training [SSR]

Steven Graham, Karen Harris, and their colleagues at the University of Maryland have developed a writing program for learning disabled students

Figure 6-2
Organization "think-sheet"

Explanations

What is being explained?

_____

In what order do things happen?

First, _____
(1st)

Then, _____
(2nd)

Then, _____
(3rd)

Then, _____
(4th)

Finally, _____
(last)

Clues: who does it, things you need, how you do it

Figure 6-3
Edit "think-sheet"

EDIT
(Explanation)

Name _____   Date _____

Read. Reread my paper.
What do I like best? (Put a * by the parts I like best)
What parts are not clear? (Put a **?** by unclear parts)

Question Yourself. Did I:

Tell what was being *explained*?	YES	sort of	NO
Tell what things you need?	YES	sort of	NO
Make the *steps* clear?	YES	sort of	NO
Use *keywords* (first, second)?	YES	sort of	NO
Make it *interesting*?	YES	sort of	NO

Plan. (look back)
What parts do I want to change?

1. _____

2. _____

Write two or more questions for my editor.

1. _____

2. _____

3. _____

Talk. (Talk to the editor.)
Read your paper with your editor. Then the editor should read the Paper and complete the Edit(or) page. Next, meet and talk about your answers.

Figure 6-4
Editor "think-sheet"

EDIT(OR) (Explanation)

Name _____ Date _____

Read. Read the paper.
What's the paper about?

_____

_____

_____

What do you like best? Put a "*" by the parts you like best.

What parts are not clear? Put a "?" by unclear parts.

Question Yourself. Did the author:

Tell what was being explained?	YES	sort of	NO
Tell what things you need?	YES	sort of	NO
Make the steps clear?	YES	sort of	NO
Use keywords (first, second)?	YES	sort of	NO
Make it interesting?	YES	sort of	NO

Plan.
What two parts would you change?

1. _____

2. _____

One thing that would make it more interesting is

_____

_____

Talk. Meet with the author.
(1) Compare your comments on the Edit and Edit(or) pages.
(2) Talk about how to fix up the paper. Help the author, if he or she
    wants help.

Figure 6-5
Revise "think-sheet"

Name _____   Date _____

1. What suggestions did your editor give?

a. _____

b. _____

c. _____

d. _____

Put a check next to the suggestions you will use.

2. How will you make your paper more interesting?

_____

_____

_____

3. Go back to your first paper and make your revisions.

REVISION SYMBOLS

Type of Revision	Symbol	Example
Add words	∧	little The girl is my sister.
Take words out	___	The woman has tried to give
Change order	∿	He had to go home
Add ideas here	⌐	The dog is friendly. Tell which dog

that includes self-instruction, self-assessment, and self-reinforcement. The program follows specific step by step instructions (See Table 6-3) and has been used to teach poor child writers how to improve their compositional skills (Harris & Graham, 1985), write better stories (Graham & Harris, 1987), write better essays (Graham & Harris, 1988a), and revise written essays (Graham & McArthur, in press). Discussion of the essay writing intervention (Graham & Harris, 1988a) illustrates the method and its effects.

The students in the program were 12 years old and were achieving two years below their age/grade level in one or more academic areas. Students were taught individually by an instructor for 45 minutes a day two or three days a week for two or three weeks. Instruction continued until students met the criteria for each step (See Table 6-3).

Step 1: Pretraining

The definition and generation of good essay components are discussed using a chart summarized by the mnemonic TREE (See Figure 6-6). After discussing the meaning of each of the prompts the student practices the mnemonic and the meaning of each of the prompts until it is memorized.

Step 2: Review Current Performance Level

The instructor and the student discuss the quality of the student's essays before the intervention begins. They then discuss the goal of the intervention (i.e., to write better essays) and why it is important. At this time a contract is filled out in which the student commits to learning the strategy for writing better essays and understands that once the course is complete, the student's best essay will be shared with the parents and the principal.

Step 3: Describe the Composition Strategy

First there is a check to determine if the student understands what it means to plan. The instructor then explains that she is going to teach a strategy that will help the student to plan and write better essays. A three-step strategy card for planning and writing is provided (See Figure 6-7).

The first part of the strategy involves thinking about who will read the essay and why the student is writing the essay. In the second step the student is taught that it is important to plan what it is that is going to be said in the essay. In order to help plan the essay, the student is instructed to use the TREE mnemonic that was learned in pretraining. For example, if the question of the essay was, "Should boys and girls play sports together?", notes would first be made summarizing the student's belief about the topic. Next, the student writes down the reasons for the beliefs that are held. During this time the use of self-statements is encouraged (e.g., Let my mind be free to think of all the reasons). Once all of the reasons have been written down, it is important for the student to examine each one. Weak reasons that would not be believed by the readers are crossed out. Then, a good ending for the essay is written. The actual writing of the essay follows, using the

Table 6-3
Self-Instructional Strategy Training

Step 1: Introduce Task-Specific Strategy (Pre-Training)
In this step a mnemonic for the strategy is introduced and its meaning mastered through various activities. The strategy is first introduced through a chart which provides a definition.

Step 2: Review Current Performance Level and Training Rationale
The instructor and the student examine how the student was performing on the targeted skill before the intervention began and discuss why training is important and how the strategy will improve performance.

Step 3: Describe the Learning Strategy
A small chart is used to introduce a learning strategy. The student is then asked to write down two or three creativity self-statements on paper and to practice using them.

Step 4: Model the Strategy and Self-Instruction
The instructor models the learning strategy (using all the necessary materials for that particular strategy), writes a story or an essay, thinking aloud as he/she does so. In thinking aloud, the instructor models not only the creativity self-statements but also self-instructions on how to (a) get started, (b) write the story, and (c) evaluate the story. The student then records examples of the self-instructional strategies that he/she would use.

Step 5: Mastery of Strategy Steps
The student is required to memorize the strategy plan. Once learned, paraphrasing of the strategy is allowed. The student is also required to memorize each type of self-instruction.

Step 6: Controlled Practice of Strategy Steps and Self-Instruction
The student practices the strategy using the visual aids, if necessary, and receives feedback from the instructor. While practicing the strategy the student is also required to use the creativity self-statements.

Step 7: Independent Performance
Students write independently, using the strategy and the self-statements. Feedback is provided and the transition to instinctive self-instruction is encouraged.

Step 8: Generalization and Maintenance Components
Students are encouraged to discuss these strategies with their parents and teachers as well as with the instructor in order to understand the benefits of using this strategy outside of the study. If necessary, behavioral contracts and cooperative planning with other teachers can be used to facilitate generalization and maintenance.

Figure 6-6
Essay parts (Self-instructional strategy training)

T - Note <u>Topic</u> Sentence

R - Note <u>Reasons</u>

E - <u>Examine</u> Reasons. Will my reader buy this?

E - Note <u>Ending</u>

Figure 6-7
3 steps for planning and writing

1. THINK
   Who?
   What?

2. PLAN
   T - Note Topic sentence
   R - Note Reasons
   E - Examine Reasons. Will my reader buy this?
   E - Note Ending

3. WRITE and SAY MORE

---

notes that were constructed previously. As the student writes, he/she may think of more things to write and should be encouraged to do so (i.e., say more).

Step 4: Model the Strategy

The three-step strategy chart is placed in front of the student and the instructor models out loud how a good essay should be written (for an example, see Table 6-4). The instructor then discusses the self-statements that were used and points out that these do not need to be spoken aloud (i.e., they can be thought of or whispered).

Step 5: Mastery of Strategy Steps

Students practice the three-step strategy and TREE until it is memorized. A procedure called *rapid fire* (a form of rote memorization) is useful in that it helps the children memorize the steps quickly. The teacher instructs the child that the purpose of this session is to memorize the steps used in writing. She then explains that the child is to say the steps as quickly as possible and, if stuck, can use the charts as a cue. The child is allowed to make use of the charts at the beginning. When the charts are removed the teacher provides prompts, as the child requires. Once the three steps have been learned, the process is repeated with TREE. The teacher makes certain that the child knows the steps and TREE, and understands them before moving to controlled practice of the strategy.

Step 6: Controlled Practice

The student and the instructor compose essays together using the three-step strategy to a) *Think*, b) *Plan*, and c) *Write and Say More*, in conjunction with the self-statements (e.g., *"Let my mind be free"* and *"Take my time"*). It should be noted that the instructor directs and monitors the progress of the student but does not actually write the essay. The strategy charts (Figure 6-6 & 6-7) are provided as prompts. When providing corrective feedback, the instructor comments on what was done incorrectly and makes certain that the student corrects the work. The teacher is positive and encouraging at all times, however.

Step 7: Independent Performance

Given a topic sentence, the student composes essays independently with corrective feedback provided by the instructor. The charts (Figures 6-6 & 6-7) are used in the beginning if necessary, but are faded by the end of this step so that the student can write an essay using the strategy independently. Practice continues until the student has demonstrated that the strategy can be used effectively.

Step 8: Generalization

The student is praised for doing a good job in learning the strategy to write better essays. The importance of using the strategy at all times is reinforced. Students are questioned on how this strategy could be used for classroom assignments. They are reminded that when writing essays, one must *Think, Plan, Write*, and *Say More*. The students are asked to share with their teacher and classmates what it was that they learned over the past few weeks.

In assessing the quality of the student essays, markers used a holistic rating scale. That is, markers read the stories and rated them for overall quality using marks of 1 to 7, with 1 being the poorest quality and 7 the highest. Samples of low, medium, and high quality essays were provided as guidelines. Graham and Harris's (1988a) program improved the quality of students' composition. The essays produced by trained students were longer and included the elements of a complete argument (i.e., premise, reasons, and conclusions). A high proportion of the information in the essays of trained students was relevant to the argument. In addition, students' perception of the criteria for a "good" essay increased.

Table 6-4
Modeling (from Graham & Harris, 1988)

Question: Is it better to be an only child or to have brothers and sisters?

OK, what is it that I have to do? I have to write an essay about whether it is better to be an only child or have brothers and sisters. First I will think about WHO and WHY. When I ask myself *who*, I am asking who will read my paper. [Name of student] will read my paper, so I will write it for him/her. Next, I need to ask myself *why*, or what is my goal. I want to do it to convince [name of student]. I want him/her to believe what I do. That's great.

I did a good job thinking about *who* and *why*. Now I will plan what I want to say. To help me plan what I want to say I will use TREE (write in keyword that goes with each letter, i.e., Topic, Reasons, Examine, Ending). First, I need to make notes for my topic sentence; I need to state what I believe. Well, I think it is better to be an only child (write note: "Better to be an only child"). Now, is this what I really believe? (pause) Yes, it is, so now I need to think of as many reasons as I can for why it is better to be an only child. I want to be sure that I can think of at least 3 or 4 reasons.

To help me think of reasons I will let my mind be free and I will take my time. (Generate 7 or 8 reasons, some good and some bad, but do not evaluate as you generate. Reinforce yourself occasionally.)

Now I need to examine the reasons to see if my reader, [name of student], will buy them. (Use student-reader as much as possible, use self-evaluative and self-reinforcement statements as much as possible, and cross out poor ideas.)

Now the last thing that I need is a good ending sentence. (Say a sentence out loud; reject the first one. Say another sentence; accept and reinforce yourself. Make notes for planning on paper.) Well, this is a good job, it will convince [name of student] that it is better to be an only child.

Now I need to use my plans to help me write my essay. As I write, I may think of other good things to say and I will want to be sure to use them in my essay. (Take out a piece of paper and write the essay while thinking out loud. Be sure to use planning, definition, evaluation, and reinforcement statements. Examples: "What do I need to do next?"; "Will my reader understand this?"; "Can I say more?"; "Great, I did a good job!")

Self-instructional strategy training has also been developed for revising (Graham & MacArthur, in press). Students are taught to self-instruct themselves to read their essay, find the sentence that tells *"what you believe,"* ask "Is it clear?", add *two reasons why they believe it*, SCAN (an acronym like TREE) each sentence and ask *"Does it make Sense?"*, *"Is it Connected to your belief?"*, *"Can you Add more?"*, *Note errors, make changes, reread essay, and make final changes*. This strategy is taught using the same eight-step plan that Graham and Harris (1988a) used, only modified for revising an essay that was already written. Evaluation of this approach revealed that this strategy increases the number of revisions and results in a much longer, better quality final product (Graham & McArthur, in press).

We emphasize that Graham and Harris (1987) believe that these strategies should not be used in a "recipe" fashion. Every student is an individual. The guidelines and the program of instruction should be tailored to the needs of each student. It should be remembered that Graham and Harris have focused on the learning disabled population in their research. This is not to say that these strategies cannot be used in regular classrooms. Rather, modifications may be necessary with average and above average readers. Certain characteristics that may determine the explicitness of instruction are age and maturity, cognitive capacity and capabilities, language development, learning style, tolerance for frustration, attitudes and expectancies, whether children already use private speech to direct their activities, and initial knowledge state and strategies that students already possess (Harris, 1985).

In a larger sense, regular classroom teachers may wish to experiment with grouping students with similar writing related performance to use this program with the small groups in thier classrooms. Future research should identify the strategy needs of the regular classroom and evaluate self instructional strategy training as part of the writing curriculum.

MICRO-STRATEGIES

The strategic interventions discussed in this chapter thus far have focused on the construction of complete essays. There are also strategies that are intended to aid only certain aspects of writing. Teachers may find these strategies helpful for children who appear to be having particular writing difficulties. Some teachers may be able to incorporate these strategies into their ongoing writing program.

Sentence Combining [SSR]

Sentence combining is a strategy that has been shown to aid children's construction of complex sentences. The main premise of sentence combining is to combine simple, related sentences into a longer, more elaborate sentence. For example, the two sentences: "Joey had a dog." and "The dog's name was Sam." could be combined to produce "Joey had a dog named Sam." Work sheets can be provided in which sentences in a paragraph are listed, with the student instructed to combine the sentences so that the paragraph flows more smoothly. Interested readers are referred to Lawlor (1983) for examples. Sentence combining improves the syntactic skills of students from grade school to college (Lawlor, 1983); that is, trained students are better at constructing complex sentences. The major problem with this strategy is that it is very narrow in its focus.

Idea Generation [T & SSR]

Many children find it hard to begin writing because they either cannot think of what to write about or, once given the topic, can think of nothing to say. Various idea generation strategies can be used in the classroom (Scardamalia & Bereiter, 1985).

Idea-generating questions have been recommended in order to get the children thinking about the types of things they could include in writing (e.g., object description, sequence of events, and arguments of the author) (Humes, 1983). (See Table 6-5 for a list of the possible questions.)

Providing *"sentence openers"* can also prompt children to think of things to write. *A sentence opener is a phrase that a writer can use to begin a sentence* (e.g., "One reason...", "Even though...", "For example...", "I think..."). Bereiter and Scardamalia (1982) discovered that children from grades 4 to 8 consistently reported that sentence openers helped them think of things to write. In providing writers with sentence openers, teachers are providing the cue to get started. This cue could either help the student who already has an idea to begin writing about it, or prompt an idea based on the sentence opener (e.g., the writer may not have thought about providing an opinion but the sentence opener "I think" provides an opportunity to do so).

Once children have identified a writing topic, it is then necessary to generate a number of pieces of information that should be included in the essay. Students can be asked to write down all the single words that they can generate that might be used in their composition. Anderson, Bereiter, and Smart (as discussed in Bereiter et al., 1982) showed that this type of training encouraged longer essays.

Planning in writing can be induced by providing an end sentence and requiring students to write a story which leads up to it. Writers must plan what they are going to write about before they begin. Tetroe (as discussed in Bereiter et al., 1982) has identified various things that writers do when using the end sentence strategy. Some children seem to adopt a "what next" approach in that as they resolve one problem raised by the ending sentence, they then continue planning the story, resolving problems along the way,

Table 6-5
Idea-Generating Questions

Describe an object
   1. What does it look like (i.e., size, shape, color)?
   2. What does it smell like?
   3. What does it sound like?
   4. What does it feel like?
   5. What does it taste like?

Sequence of Events
   1. What happened first?*
   2. What happened next? Next?*
   3. What happened last?*
   4. When did it happen?
   5. Where did it happen?
   6. Whom did it happen to?

Facts on a Topic
   1. What is the topic?
   2. Why is the topic important?
   3. What part of the topic should I write about?
   4. How can I illustrate the topic?
   5. What other questions can I ask about the topic?
   6. What are the answers to these questions?
   7. Do I have any problems with this topic?
   8. What are the solutions to these problems?

Arguments or Opinions
   1. What opinion can a person have about this topic?
   2. Which of them is my opinion?
   3. What reasons can others have about this topic?
   4. What reasons can I give them to show that my opinion is right?
   5. What can I say to prove my reason is a good reason?

* For older children, these three questions can be replaced by the following two questions:

1. What is the problem?
2. What is the solution to the problem?

From Humes, 1983

one at a time. Other students have been shown to make decisions in light of all the constraints posed by the ending sentence before they begin writing. A third technique can be used when the end sentence imposes too few constraints. In this case, the child can sidestep the issue. For example, "The captain of the spaceship said that they would never visit that planet again" can cue the child to write a story about a spaceship or develop the theme that there was a problem on the planet that would prevent anyone from ever going back. In providing too few constraints, the teacher only gives the student a topic for the passage. On the other hand, a sentence such as "The fireman decided to keep the dog in spite of the trouble that he had caused" forces the writer to relate a fireman, a dog, and trouble, taking a number of constraints into account.

Generating More Text [T & SSR]

It has been found that a lot of student writers stop their writing when they still have more ideas to convey. It seems that the main problem in generating content is accessing and giving order to ideas (Bereiter et al., 1982). The writer does not have the verbal feedback of an audience who can prompt access to additional ideas (McCutchen et al., 1983; Scardamalia et al., 1986). When teachers prompt children to write more by asking them to clarify an idea, or by simply advising them to write more, children do in fact write more (Scardamalia et al., 1985). This simple strategy may be helpful with students who are prematurely ending their compositions. At first the prompt may come from the teacher but eventually, with guidance, the student should be able to internalize a self-instruction to write more (especially if instructed to do so; e.g., Graham & Harris, 1987), and thus produce more elaborate written material.

Revision of Text [SSR]

Students spend very little time on revision. When it is done, it often harms the paper rather than improves it (Bracewell, Scardamalia, & Bereiter, 1978). An important distinction here is between rewriting and revising a text (Hayes et al., 1987). In order to assess which may be appropriate, Hayes and Flower (1987) provide some guidelines:

Rewrite if:
• it is not important to save the original text,
• there are so many problems with the original text that diagnosing the problem would waste more time than rewriting, or
• the purpose of the text is clear, so that extracting an idea and writing a new text with this idea is easy.

Revise if:
- it is important to save as much of the original text as possible,
- the diagnosis of the errors is easy, or
- the purpose of the text is unclear, so extracting an idea and using it to rewrite the text is not possible.

Once it has been decided that the writing should be revised there are a number of interventions that a teacher might employ.

Scardamalia and Bereiter (1983) developed a procedure referred to as "C.D.O." (*compare, diagnose, operate*). C.D.O. has been taught to grade 4, 6, and 8 children. It requires approximately 90 minutes to teach, using one of two instructional approaches.

The first approach is *on-line revision*, revising each sentence as it is written. There are two sets of questions the writer asks after a sentence is written (See Table 6-6). The writer first poses evaluative questions to ensure the sentence is a valuable one. Having evaluated the sentence, the writer then turns to the directives displayed in Table 6-6. Based upon the evaluation of the sentence, the writer chooses one of the six directives and either leaves the sentence as it is or changes it. In instructing revision using this strategy, the teacher should provide examples and use verbal modeling so students understand what each evaluation and directive involves.

The second approach was *"evaluation after."* The questions used in "on-line" revision were used, except that revision occurred after the paragraph was complete. This seems like a more realistic way of teaching, since few people write and revise one sentence at a time.

Scardamalia and Bereiter found that none of the children they studied were unwilling or unable to use the C.D.O. strategy. For grade 4 and 6 children, there was no difference in the length of the papers produced by the *"on-line"* or *"evaluation after"* techniques. However, for grade 8 children the "evaluation after" technique produced longer papers than the "on-line" technique. There were mixed reactions regarding how the children felt about the C.D.O. strategy. Generally, 74% of the students thought that this strategy made writing easier, because it made them think of questions that they had never thought of before. Twelve percent of the students felt it made writing harder, because they needed to think more carefully, and it took longer to write.

Unfortunately, paragraphs revised with the C.D.O. approach were not judged to be any better (or worse) than the originals. There were, however, a number of potential reasons for this. First, there were negative changes made by the students (i.e., they changed things that should not have been revised). Second, the evaluative phrases "I'm getting away from the main point" and "Even I'm confused about what I'm saying" were not chosen with any high frequency. In fact the statement "I think I'll leave it the way that it is" was chosen 49.5% to 68.3% of the time. This would suggest that although children can be taught to ask these questions, they are not aware of what to do with them and still have difficulties in deciding what to revise.

Table 6-6
Evaluations and Directives Used in CDO

Evaluative Phrases
1. People won't see why this is important.
2. People may not believe this.
3. People won't be very interested in this part.
4. People may not understand what I mean here.
5. People will be interested in this part.
6. This is good.
7. This is a useful sentence.
8. I think that this could be said more clearly.
9. I'm getting away from the main point.
10. Even I am confused about what I'm trying to say.
11. This doesn't sound quite right.

Directive Phrases
1. I think I'll leave it this way.
2. I'd better give an example.
3. I'd better leave this part out.
4. I'd better cross this sentence out and say it differently.
5. I'd better say more.
6. I'd better change this wording.

From Scardamalia et al., 1983

Merely telling students what to do and showing them once is not enough to get them to revise adequately. It is for this reason that Fitzgerald and Markham (1987) have developed a strategy that involves more direct instruction of revision.

Fitzgerald and Markham (1987) taught average writers in grade 6 to revise during thirteen 45-minute lessons over a one month period. There were four 3-day cycles, with day 13 being a review of the previous 12 sessions. Each cycle focused on one of the four types of revision: *additions, deletions, substitutions, and rearrangements* (Faigley & Witte, 1981). The instructions for the group centered on teaching revision as a problem solving process. In this way the teacher modeled detecting mismatches between written and intended text, decided how to change this text, and then changed it. On Day 1 of each cycle, the teacher referred to the chart describing the type of revision to be discussed. She then used think-alouds to model the revision strategy to the children. After this, the class practiced revision. On Day 2, the material from Day 1 was reviewed, and the children worked in pairs revising a portion of text by using a handout that led them through the problem solving process of revision. The children then wrote a brief story. Day 3 also included review. Then the children revised a portion of a story given to them by a teacher. They also revised the story that they had written the day before. Throughout all lessons, the children were taught to think of revising as a problem solving process. (For an example of a typical cycle see Table 6-7.)

Fitzgerald and Markham (1987) found that their program led sixth grade children to identify discrepancies between written and intended text and to be specific in identifying the changes that needed to be made. Compared to children not instructed about revision, trained children made more revisions, and the quality of their papers increased throughout the program. Unfortunately, the final quality of the essays was not, on average, strikingly better than the quality of the non-trained students' essays after the same period of time.

In short, revision strategies are being devised and tested. The tactics studied to date have failed to improve overall writing performance beyond the level of non-trained control students, although more subtle changes in literary skills have been obtained. The importance of revision will motivate more work on the topic. Very few first drafts would not benefit from effective revision. In fact, many revisions would benefit from additional, more effective revisions.

COMPUTERS AND COMPOSITION [T]

Composing on the word processor differs from handwriting in a number of ways that may affect the composition. First, word processors permit flexible editing of text. Second, the visibility of the monitor and the text make writing more public. Third, word processors provide neat, printed copies. Fourth, they replace handwriting with keypunching. Finally, word processors are complex tools, which require some learning (MacArthur, 1988). Since there are differences between handwriting and word processing, it may not be too surprising that there are differences in the length of handwritten and word processed student papers (Collier, 1983; Dauite, 1986), the number of revisions (Collier, 1983), and attitudes toward writing, all favoring the word processor. The Hawthorne effect (i.e., doing well because of the novelty of the exercise) might explain some of these differences. Alternatively, the computer seems like a "mature" thing to be working on, and student writers might be motivated to write well on the computer for that reason (Dauite, 1985).

The computer is not a quick fix for composing, however, and merely letting children use it without providing strategies for writing is not going to improve writing quality very much. This may be comforting to teachers who feel left behind because their school cannot afford computers.

Our reserved opinion of the word processor as a facilitator of writing is

**Table 6-7
Revision**

Introduction:
The teacher explains that revisions means to identify problems, make decisions about how to change the text, and have knowledge on how to make these changes.

Modeling Stage (Day 1)
The teacher first announces that there will be revisions made to various parts of the composition and while making these revisions the teacher will talk out loud so that the students can see how she thinks. While the transparency of the composition to be revised is presented to the children the teacher may say the following:

"Let's say I've written this story. Now I think to myself I want my readers to have an eerie feeling about what happened to the husband and the brothers. My goal is to add mystery and make my readers feel uncomfortable. I think this part where it says 'left and never came back' isn't mysterious or eerie." (The teacher points to "locate a problem" on the chart and says "This is locating a problem.") "Now I think to myself, how could I change it?" (The teacher then describes possible ways to change the passage.)

The teacher then points to "Decision: Decide how it could or should be changed" on the chart and says: "This is deciding how it can be fixed."

The teacher then explains that once the decision about what to add has been made it is time to "Change: Make the change." Finally, the teacher summarizes the problem-solving way of thinking about revision, reiterating that writers locate problems, decide how to make changes, and actually make changes on paper.

Guided Practice (Day 2)
With the help of the teacher, the students attempt to practice their revision strategy and to share their experiences by working in pairs. A handout is given to the children outlining what they learned on day one to help them through the revision process. The text to be revised should be rigged such that there is ample room for revision. If the area of concentration is addition, then there should be a stress on additions; if the concentration is on deletions, then there should be plenty to delete, etc. After the pairs are finished, the class shares their revisions. During the discussion it is important that the reasons the children made the changes that they did be discussed. At the end of the session the teacher then reviews the problem solving approach to revision.

Independent Application (Day 3)
First, the students individually revise a passage given to them by the teacher. Finally, the students write and revise their own compositions.

From Fitzgerald & Markham, in press

reinforced by data produced in the 1930's on a new machine for word processing: the typewriter. Wood and Freeman (as cited in Pea & Kurland, 1987) studied 2,383 students over two years of writing as they learned to write on typewriters. They observed that the students using the typewriters wrote longer compositions with more expression, had advanced reading scores, became better spellers, and expressed a greater interest and enjoyment in writing stories. These conclusions are similar to the conclusions that are being made in studies of microcomputers versus handwriting (e.g., Dauite, 1985; Glebe, 1987; Rodrigues, 1985). Unfortunately, skilled writing requires more, including processes encouraged by the strategies reviewed in this chapter.

Conclusion

We conclude with recommendations made by Graham and Harris (1988b) for implementing a writing program in the classroom:

1. Write at least four times a week (i.e., allocate time).
2. Expose students to a broad range of writing tasks.
3. Create a social climate conducive to writing.
4. Integrate writing with other academic subjects.
5. Aid students in developing the processes central to writing—that is, the three recursive processes identified by Flower and Hayes (1980); planning, translating, and reviewing should be taught as well as the task specific and metacognitive strategies outlined previously.
6. Automatize the skills for getting language onto paper. If writers have not mastered the techniques of spelling, punctuation, and sentence production, these lower-level writing elements can interfere with higher cognitive processes such as content generation. Direct instruction of lower-level skills is helpful, in that once they become automatized, writers can perform them with little conscious attention (i.e., this "frees" their attention for higher-level aspects of writing).
7. Writing programs should include examples of various writings (e.g. narrative and expository) so that students can learn the attributes of various types of writing.
8. Help students develop the skills and abilities to carry out more sophisticated composing processes. This can be accomplished by teaching writers the various strategies outlined in this chapter.
9. Assist students in the development of goals for improving their written products.
10. Avoid instructional practices that do not improve students' writing performance. Systematic teaching of grammar and usage and *overemphasis* on low-level writing errors (e.g., spelling, punctuation) do not help. Although instruction in low-level skills is important, they should

not be taught in isolation. Persistent attention to low-level errors is probably especially harmful. It tends to make students focus on their shortcomings rather than on their strengths (Hillocks, 1984) and thus has the potential for undermining motivation to write. In contrast, most of the procedures reviewed in this chapter should enhance motivation to write.

REFERENCES

Anthony, K.M., Gregg, S.L., & Englert, C.S. (1987). *Implementinq cognitive strategy instruction: Impact on elementary students' composition and comprehension of expository text.* Paper presented at the National Reading Conference, St. Petersburg Beach, Florida.

Applebee, A.N. (1981). Looking at writing. *Educational Leadership, 38,* 458-462.

Applebee, A.N. (1982). Writing and learning in school settings. In M. Nystrand (Ed.), *What writers know: The language process and structure of written discourse.* New York: Academic Press.

Bereiter, C., & Scardamalia, M. (1982). From conversation to composition: The role of instruction in a developmental process. In R. Glaser (Ed.), *Advances in instructional psychology* (Vol. 2, pp. 1-64). Hillsdale, NJ: Lawrence Erlbaum Associates.

Bos, C.S. (1988). Process oriented writing: Instructional implications for mildly handicapped students. *Exceptional Children, 54,* 521-527.

Bracewell, R.J., Scardamalia, M., & Bereiter, C. (1978). The development of audience awareness in writing. *Resources in Education* (October, ERIC Document Reproduction Services No. ED 154 443).

Collier, R.M. (1983). The word processor and revision strategies. *College Composition and Communication, 34,* 149-155.

Dauite, C.A. (1985). *Writing and computers.* New York: Addison-Wesley.

Dauite, C.A. (1986). Physical and cognitive factors in revising. Insights from students with computers. *Research in the Teaching of English, 20,* 141-158.

Dominic, J.F. (1983). Research on writing: A response. *The Elementary School Journal, 84,* 88-92.

Englert, C.S., & Raphael, T.C. (1988). Constructing well formed prose: Process, structure, and metacognitive knowledge. *Exceptional Children, 54,* 513-520.

Englert, C.S., & Raphael, T.E. (in press). Developing successful writers through cognitive strategy instruction. In J.E. Brophy (Ed.), *Advances in research on teaching.* JAI Press.

Faigley, L., & Witte, S. (1981). Analyzing revision. *Colleqe Composition and Communication, 32*, 400-414.

Fitzgerald, J., & Markham, L.R. (1987). Teaching children about revision in writing. *Cognition and Instruction, 4*, 3-24.

Fitzgerald, J., & Markham, L.R. (in press). Helping students revise their writing. *Middle School Journal.*

Fitzgerald, J., & Teasley, A.B. (1986). Effects of instruction in narrative structure on children's writing. *Journal of Educational Psychology, 78*, 424-432.

Flower, L.S., & Hayes, J.R. (1980). Identifying the organization of writing processes. In L.W. Gregg & E.R. Steinberg (Eds.), *Cognitive processes in writing* (pp. 3-30). Hillsdale, NJ: Lawrence Erlbaum Associates.

Glebe, D. (1987). *A computer study of handwritten stories vs. stories written on the computer by elementary school children.* Unpublished M.Ed. thesis. Faculty of Education, The University of Western Ontario.

Graham, S., & Harris, K.R. (1987). *A components analysis of cognitive strategy training: Effects on learning disabled students' compositions and self-efficacy.* Manuscript submitted for publication.

Graham, S., & Harris, K.R. (1988a). *Improving learning disabled students' skills at generating essays: Self-instructional strategy instruction.* Manuscript submitted for publication.

Graham, S., & Harris, K.R. (1988b). Instructional recommendations for teaching writing to exceptional students. *Exceptional Children, 54*, 506-512.

Graham, S., & McArthur, C. (in press). Improving learning disabled students' skills at revising essays produced on a word processor: Self-instructional strategy training. *Journal of Special Education.*

Harris, K.R. (1985). Conceptual, methodological, and clinical issues in cognitive behavioral assessment. *Journal of Abnormal Child Psychology, 13*, 373-390.

Harris, K.R., & Graham, S. (1985). Improving learning disabled students' composition skills: Self-control strategy training. *Learning Disability Quarterly, 8*, 27-36.

Hayes, J.R., & Flower, L.S. (1986). Writing research and the writer. *American Psychologist, 41*, 1106-1113.

Hayes, J.R., & Flower, L.S. (1987). On the structure of the writing process. *Topics in Language Disorders, 7,* 19-30.

Hillocks, G. (1984). What works in teaching composition: A meta-analysis of experimental treatment studies. *American Journal of Education, 93,* 133-170.

Humes, A. (1983). Putting writing research into practice. *The Elementary School Journal, 84,* 53-62.

Lawlor, J. (1983). Sentence combining: A sequence for instruction. *The Elementary School Journal, 84,* 53-62.

McArthur, C. (1988). The impact of computers on the writing process. *Exceptional Children, 54,* 536-542.

McCutchen, D., & Perfetti, C.A. (1983). Local coherence: Helping young writers manage a complex task. *The Elementary School Journal, 84,* 71-75.

Odell, L. (1980). Teaching writing by the process of discovery. In L.W. Gregg & E.R. Steinberg (Eds.), *Cognitive processes in writing.* Hillsdale, NJ: Lawrence Erlbaum Associates.

Pea, R.D., & Kirkland, D.M. (1987). Cognitive technologies for writing. *Review of Research in Education, 14,* 277-326.

Perl, S. (1983). How teachers teach the writing process. *The Elementary School Journal, 84,* 19-24.

Raphael, T.C., Englert, C.S., & Anderson, L.M. (1987). *What is effective in writinq instruction: A comparison of two writing lessons.* Paper presented at the National Reading Conference, St. Petersburg, Florida.

Rodrigues, D. (1985). Composition and basic writers. *College Composition and Communication, 36,* 336-339.

Rohman, G. (1965). Pre-writing: The stage of discovery in the writing process. *College Composition and Communication, 16,* 106-112.

Scardamalia, M. (1981). How children cope with the cognitive demands of writing. In C.H. Frederiksen, M.F. Whiteman, & J.F. Dominic (Eds.), *Writing: The nature, development. and teaching of written communication.* Hillsdale, NJ: Lawrence Erlbaum Associates.

Scardamalia, M., & Bereiter, C. (1983). The development of evaluative, diagnostic, and remedial capabilities in children's composing. In M.

Martlew (Ed.), *The psychology of written language* (pp. 67-95). London: Wiley.

Scardamalia, M., & Bereiter, C. (1985). Research on written composition. In M. Wittrock (Ed.), *Handbook of research on teaching* (3rd Edition, pp 778-803). New York: MacMillan.

Stevens, D.D., Anthony, K.M., & Englert, C.S. (1988). *The effects of cognitive strategy instruction in writing on the expository reading/writing performance of special education students.* Paper presented at the Annual Meeting of the Council for Exceptional Children, Washington, D.C.

Stevens, P., & Fear, K.L. (1987). *Metacognitive knowledge about writing informational text: Effects of cognitive strategy instruction.* Paper presented at the National Reading Conference, St. Petersburg, Florida.

Wilkinson, A.C. (1983). *Classroom computers and cognitive science.* New York: Academic Press.

Wresch, W. (1987). *A practical guide to computer uses in the English/lanquaqe arts classroom.* Englewood Cliffs, NJ: Prentice Hall.

CHAPTER 7

Mathematics

This chapter reviews research relating to strategies for mathematical computation and problem solving, with problem solving conceptualized as it was by Polya (1957), who proposed four stages in the solution of a problem: (1) understanding the problem, (2) devising a plan, (3) carrying out the plan, and (4) looking back. According to Polya, the first of these stages involves translating the problem into a manageable version. This process may require restatement of the problem and explicit identification of the principal parts of the problem (the unknown, the data, and the problem conditions). Devising a plan requires determining both the operations that will be used in the solution of the problem and the order in which those operations will be carried out. Devising the plan is a necessary prerequisite to the third stage of problem solving, which is carrying out the plan. This stage involves performing the computations planned in the second step. The fourth and final stage of problem solving, looking back, involves re-examining the solution and the method that led to this solution. This step is critical in the consolidation of knowledge and the development of the ability to solve problems. It is at this stage that the problem solver can pose the following question: "Can I use the result or the method for some other problem?" (see Table 7-1). All of the strategies covered in this chapter can be discussed in the context of Polya's general problem-solving approach.

The primary purpose of this chapter is to present empirical evidence concerning the efficacy of strategy instruction for enhancing math performance. Ideally, we would present an analysis of various individual strategies, with each including a description of prerequisite knowledge, evidence that the strategies can be taught, evidence that problem solving performance improves with use of the strategies, and detailed methodologies for teaching each strategy. Unfortunately, there are few if any empirical studies which investigate a single strategy so thoroughly. Instead, subjects are usually taught a constellation of strategies to employ in problem-solving situations. As a result, it is impossible to isolate the specific strategies which are most effective. A related problem with the research is the lack of detail provided about strategies that are taught or how they are instructed. For example, although a study might report that subjects were taught to paraphrase problems, it might fail to include a detailed description of the instruction designed to teach this strategy. There are rarely specific examples of strategy use included in these reports. Finally, most studies do not determine whether strategy training actually produces commitment to strategy use. In other words, there are no explicit measures to assess which, if any, of the trained strategies are correctly employed by students. Thus, even in cases where strategy instruction improves performance, it is not always clear that the improvement is the direct result of strategy use.

These limitations in the research dictated a particular approach to the evaluation of this literature. There is a review of a number of strategy instructional studies in this chapter, including discussion of the strategies used, their instructional methods, and results of the strategy training. Subsequently, those strategies and teaching principles common to successful strategy instruction approaches are considered in more detail. Finally, recommendations for strategy instruction based on Polya's four-stage model follow from this review of the literature. The discussion proceeds from strategies for basic mathematics to those that are directed at more advanced problem solving.

Table 7-1
Polya's Four-Stage Model

Stage 1: Understanding the Problem
What are you looking for?
What information is given in the problem?
Draw a diagram.

Stage 2: Devising a Plan
Do you know a similar problem?
Do you know an easier problem?
Can you restate the problem?
Try to solve a related problem.
Try to solve part of the problem.

Stage 3: Carrying out the Plan
Carry out the plan of the solution, checking each step.
Can you prove each step is correct?

Stage 4: Looking Back
Check the calculations and result.
Can you get the result using a different method?
Can you use this result for another problem?

From *How to Solve It* (p. XVI, XVII) by G. Polya, 1957, Garden City, NY: Doubleday Anchor Books. Copyright 1957 by G. Polya. Adapted by permission.

Basic Mathematics

A general consideration in any strategy instruction is that of prerequisite knowledge (e.g., Pressley, Borkowski, & Schneider, 1987). The situation is no different in mathematics strategy instruction; knowledge of basic math facts and operations is required for any problem solving in mathematics. There is an ongoing debate whether children learn basic math facts through recall or through derivation (computation). Some authors (e.g., Ashcraft, 1985) suggest that recall is the usual method (i.e., children have stored the answers to basic math problems in long-term memory) with derivation as a backup in cases where the fact is not available for recall (e.g., for 3 + 5, the child begins with 5 and counts upwards three digits to 8). Others (e.g., Baroody, 1985) believe that derivation is the usual method, and recall is used only in the case of the most familiar facts. Recall and derivation demand different educational approaches. Drill and practice is suggested as the best method to encourage encoding of math facts into long-term memory so that they can be recalled automatically later, while strategy instruction is an obvious method of improving math fact derivation.

As Wood and Dunlap (1982) point out, however, drill and practice is most effective when it follows mathematics instruction aimed at building understanding and meaning (see also Rathmell, 1978). Thus, it is not surprising that strategies for learning math facts often include emphasis on understanding of mathematical relationships.

Thornton (1978) investigated the effects of strategy instruction on the acquisition of basic addition, subtraction, multiplication, and division facts. Grade 2 students (22 control, 25 thinking strategy) were instructed in addition and subtraction facts while grade 4 students (20 control, 23 thinking strategy) were instructed in multiplication and division. The duration of instruction was 8 weeks. For all types of instruction, teachers met with the investigators several times both before and during the study. Before the study began, the grade 2 controls outperformed experimental subjects on an addition and subtraction test; the multiplication and division performances of trained and control grade 4 subjects were equivalent on the pretest.

The teachers of the grade 2 and grade 4 control groups followed the traditional teaching approach. The thinking strategies groups were taught the addition and multiplication facts in a particular order [T], designated by the investigator. The order of presentation was designed to emphasize the relation of harder facts to easier known ones.

For addition facts, the order was: doubles (e.g. 5 + 5); doubles + 1 (e.g. 5 + 6); "sharing numbers," which differ by two, and can be related to doubles by subtracting one from the larger addend and adding one to the smaller addend (e.g. 6 + 8); additions to 9, whose result is one less than adding 10 to a number (e.g. 9 + 5), and finally the 10 facts not covered under any of these categories (e.g. 2 + 5). Table 7-2 presents examples of the addition strategies, with explanations.

Multiplication facts were presented in the following order: products of

2's (e.g. 2 x 8); products of 5's (e.g. 5 x 4); products of nines (e.g. 9 x 7); squares (e.g. 4 x 4) and the 10 facts not included in any of these categories (e.g. 3 x 4).

To solve subtraction and division problems, strategy-trained participants were encouraged to think of the related addition or multiplication fact; this was the only strategy taught for the subtraction and division facts.

The posttests, administered immediately following the 8 weeks of instruction, and the retention tests, administered two weeks after the termination of instruction, were identical to the pretests. The thinking skills students outperformed the control groups on the posttest for all mathematical operations (addition and subtraction at the grade 2 level, and multiplication and division at the grade 4 level). The advantage of the thinking skills instruction was also evident at the retention test. Thus, the thinking skills training led to better performance on addition, subtraction, multiplication, and division basic facts.

Steinberg (1985) provided an uncontrolled pretest-to-posttest study that complemented Thornton's (1978) work. She investigated how well grade 2 children (23 students) used derived-facts strategies (DFSs) (strategies that relate unknown facts to easier, known facts) once they had received instruction in these strategies for addition and subtraction. Instruction occurred for eight weeks. The presentation of facts was almost identical to Thornton (1978) with the following exceptions. In addition to "doubles + 1" and "doubles - 1," Steinberg taught two analogous strategies of "doubles + 2" and "doubles - 2" (an example is 6 + 8 solved as [6 + 6 = 12] + 2 =14). Furthermore, she does not treat "addition to 9" as a separate strategy. Instead, she uses a "going through 10" strategy that relates number facts to the number 10. Thus, to solve the problem 8 + 5 the student is encouraged to think (8 + 2 = 10) + 3 = 13. Addition facts that include 9 as one of the addends are taught first, as the easiest cases of the "going through 10" strategy. As in the Thornton (1978) study, the strategy for subtraction involved relating the subtraction fact to the appropriate addition fact. For example, to solve 12 - 6, the student is taught to think of what adds to 6 to get 12. See Table 7-2 for examples of the strategies and their use.

In order to determine how children solve addition and subtraction problems, the investigator interviewed each of the 23 participants a total of four times. The first interview, identical in structure to the third and fourth interviews, consisted of five word problems and eight addition and five subtraction number combinations; the word problems were omitted from the second interview. The interview format permitted the investigator to observe and listen to the children solve the problems. In addition, a short timed test of addition and subtraction facts was administered at each of the three interviews. The first interview occurred prior to instruction, the second midway through instruction, the third immediately following instruction, and the fourth was approximately one month after instruction had terminated. The use of derived-facts strategies resulted in a significant increase between the first and second interview, but no significant increase was noted between the second and third interview. Furthermore, the

Table 7-2
Addition Strategies

Name	Example	Description
Doubles	5 + 5 = 10	Basic facts for strategy use - to be memorized
Doubles + 1 or Doubles - 1	5 + 6 = 11	Double the smaller digit and add 1, or double the larger digit and subtract 1:
	5 + 6 = 5 + (5 + 1) (5 + 5 = 10) + 1 =11 or 5 + 6 = (6 - 1) + 6 (6 + 6 = 12) - 1 = 11	
Doubles + 2 or Doubles - 2	5 + 7 = 12	Double the smaller digit and add 2, or double the larger digit and subtract 2:
	5 + 7 = 5 + (5 + 2) (5 + 5 = 10) +2 = 12 or 5 + 7 = (7 - 2) + 7 (7 + 7 = 14) - 2 = 12	
Sharing	6 + 8 = 14	Subtract one from the larger addend, and add one to the smaller addend to create a double:
	(6 + 1 = 7) + (8 - 1 = 7) 7 + 7 = 14	
Addition with 9 or Going through 10	9 + 5 = 14 8 + 5 = 13	Use one of the addends and part of the other to add to 10; then add the remainder of the second addend:
	(9 + 1 = 10) + (5 - 1 = 4) 10 + 4 = 14 or (8 + 2 = 10) + (5 - 2 = 3) 10 + 3 = 13	

proportion of correct answers to both addition and subtraction problems increased from the first to the second timed test, while the proportion of correct answers to subtraction problems significantly increased from the second to the third timed test. The primary contribution of this study was to show that grade 2 students are capable of using and will use strategies for basic addition and subtraction facts.

Lloyd, Saltzman, and Kauffman (1981) studied strategy training for the acquisition of basic multiplication and division facts with grade 3 learning disabled children. Four students were involved in this study, with the investigators able to demonstrate pretest-to-posttest gains following strategy instruction. Unfortunately, like Steinberg's (1985) study, Lloyd et al.'s (1981) research did not include uninstructed control participants. The training involved three phases: $[T + SSR]$ preskills training followed by two sessions of strategy training. During preskills instruction, students performed rote counting sequences for six numbers, in the following order: 5's, 7's, 2's, 10's, 3's, and 4's. Each sequence began with 0, and then counted by the designated number 10 times. For example, the counting sequence taught for three is: 0, 3, 6, 9, 12, 15, 18, 21, 24, 27, 30. Training in this preskills phase was accomplished in two ways. First, the trainer modeled the correct chain and the children repeated it several times with the trainer while the trainer faded his or her prompting. In the second method, a chain was written on the blackboard and the children read each number out loud as the trainer pointed to it. Once the children had successfully read each number, the trainer systematically erased numbers from the chain and the children were required to fill in the blanks as they read the chain.

Pre-skills training procedures were repeated daily for approximately 5 to 10 minutes with each child. It took approximately 20 days to reach mastery of the number sequences, indicated by the ability to recite all counting sequences without error on two consecutive trials for two different trainers on two consecutive days.

Strategy training was conducted twice: immediately following successful pre-skills training and the day after the end of pre-skills training. For both days, training lasted approximately 20 to 25 minutes. The strategy included: (1) pointing to a number "you can count by," (2) making hash marks for the other number, (3) counting by "the number you pointed to," once for each hash mark, and (4) writing in the answer space "the last number you said." This strategy was modelled; then the child was instructed to repeat the steps of the strategy aloud as the trainer solved another problem. Finally, the children solved problems on their own.

Multiplication ability was assessed at the beginning of each session using a short untimed test that included several basic multiplication problems. Performance for solving basic multiplication problems increased markedly during training. (Because of the small number of subjects, no statistical analysis was conducted.)

In a second experiment, using only three of the original four subjects, the authors investigated the use of a skip counting strategy for division $[T+SSR]$.

The design was similar to the first experiment, although pretraining was not required since students had learned the counting sequences in the previous study. Students were individually trained in a single session lasting 110 minutes. First, they were taught to recognize the division sign. They were then taught the strategy for division, which involved counting by the divisor until the dividend is reached and making hash marks as each number in the counting sequence was verbalized. When the dividend was reached using skip counting, the number of hash marks was counted, providing the correct answer to the problem. Children practiced the strategy on nineteen problems. Strategy training produced improved performance on division problems, as assessed by sets of three problems administered every nine minutes through the session. There was no evidence that the division strategy interfered with the multiplication strategy that was taught previously.

Complex Math Problem Solving

The more sophisticated strategies required to solve complex addition, subtraction, multiplication, and division problems (i.e. multi-digit problems) have also been investigated. In a large scale study preparing learning disabled students for a competency math test, Hargest, Wood, Rose, and Coughlin (1980) instructed 7th and 8th grade learning disabled students in math strategies [SSR]. Their math strategy instruction focused on number concepts, whole number operations, fraction operations, measurement, using data, and problem solving. Their sample included four resource classrooms. In two of these classes the students were taught the learning strategies while the two control classes received regular instruction. The treatment lasted for an entire school year, beginning with a pretest to determine the exact skill and/or strategy deficiencies responsible for each student's poor performance. If it was determined that a student was skill deficient, instruction in the underdeveloped skill preceded strategy instruction. Strategy instruction explicitly followed the model developed by Deshler, Alley, Warner, and Schumacker (1981). For each of the four operations (addition, subtraction, multiplication, and division), instruction involved three steps. In the first step, students were taught the skill and the strategy was described. In the second step, the strategy was modelled by the instructor. Finally, students verbally rehearsed the strategy steps. Table 7-3 contains the strategy steps for each of the four operations. The learning strategy intervention improved math performance. Unfortunately, the math strategies were not analyzed individually for effectiveness.

It is cause for optimism that research continues on the development of strategies for more complex computations. For instance, in an uncontrolled pretest-posttest design, Rivera and Smith (1988) developed and provided preliminary evaluation of a keyword strategy for long division [SSR]. Their subjects were eight learning disabled students enrolled in middle school. The strategy included: (1) the teacher demonstrates the solution of a sample problem while verbalizing keywords for the steps used, (2) the student models the process using a sample problem while repeating the keywords, and (3) the student completes a worksheet using the demonstrated problem as a referent. Table 7-4 shows the solution of a sample division problem and the keywords associated with each step. Students received math instruction four days per week; each strategy-instruction session was identical (as described above), averaging 10 minutes as part of a 45-minute math class. The remainder of the math lesson was spent completing the individual division worksheets.

Each student received from 2 to 9 days of strategy instruction, depending on when they reached the criterion performance of 100% correct on two successive worksheets. During independent work time (completing worksheets), instructors circulated among the students, providing appropriate key questions to any students who were having difficulties. The key questions were "What is the problem?" "What are the steps?" "What did you just do?" and "What do you do next?" The teacher did not provide the answers to the key questions, and the division process was not demonstrated again that day.

Quantitative analysis of the results of the strategy intervention was not performed. However, a comparison of performance on division worksheets prior to instruction (the baseline measure) with performance during instruction (all instructional sessions up to and including the two 100% worksheets required to reach criterion) revealed that, for every student, overall performance was better during instruction.

Summary

There are a number of effective strategies for learning both basic math facts and the algorithms for the mathematical operations of addition, subtraction, multiplication, and division. Conceptual approaches encourage students to relate new facts to previously-known facts. Thus, for addition, students are first taught the "doubles" (e.g., 4 + 4), and then taught to solve "doubles + 1" (e.g., 4 + 5) by relating these facts to the associated "double." Multiplication fact strategies are similar in relating new facts to previously known ones. Strategies taught for subtraction and division involve instructing students to relate subtraction and division facts to the associated addition or multiplication fact. Thus, for example, the strategy for learning the fact 4 - 2 = 2 involves remembering that 2 + 2 = 4.

Strategies for multi-digit computations assume knowledge of the basic (single-digit) math facts. In general, most of the strategies investigated to date are of the keyword (or "key phrase") type. Students memorize a series of explicit steps in solving multi-digit problems. For addition, the strategy

Table 7-3
Strategy Instruction for Four Operations

Operation	Strategy Steps
Addition	1. Add down 2. Carry if needed 3. Repeat next column

Subtraction	1. Start with ones column
	2. Look at top number
	    Top number larger or same?
	    Subtract
	    Top number smaller?
	    Borrow and rename
	3. Repeat next column

Multiplication One-digit multiplier	1. Multiply bottom number and ones digit 2. Carry, if needed 3. Multiply bottom number and tens digit and add carried number 4. Repeat
Multiplication Two-digit multiplier	1. Multiply bottom ones digit and top number 2. Write zero as place holder 3. Multiply bottom tens digit and top number 4. Add
Division One-digit divisor	1. Divide 2. Multiply 3. Subtract and compare 4. Bring down one digit 5. Repeat
Division Two-digit divisor	1. Estimate 2. Divide 3. Multiply 4. Subtract and compare 5. Bring down one digit 6. Repeat

From *A Learning Strategies Approach to Functional Mathematics for Students with Special Needs: A Special Education Instructional Guide* (pp. 52, 59, 66, 81). Bel Air, MD: Harford County Public Schools. Adapted by permission.

Table 7-4
Example of a Keyword Strategy

SAMPLE PROBLEM: 1240 DIVIDED BY 5

Self Questions and Prompts	Key Words
Does 5 go into 1? No. Does 5 go into 12? Yes.	Go into?
Place dot (for reminder): 12.40	Place dot
How many times does 5 go into 12?	Divide
Multiply: 5 x 2	Multiply
Subtract: 12 - 10	Subtract
Check. Is the subtraction answer smaller than the divisor? (Is 12 - 10 less than 5?) If "yes," continue. If "no," check work.	Check
Bring down the next number.	Bring down
Repeat until there are no more numbers to bring down.	Repeat
Put up remainder, even if it's 0.	Put up remainder

From "Using a Demonstration Strategy to Teach Midschool Students with Learning Disabilities How to Compute Long Division" by D. Rivera and D.D. Smith, 1988, *Journal of Learning Disabilities, 21*, p. 77-81. Copyright 1988 by PRO-ED Inc. Adapted by permission.

consists of exact instructions about the order in which columns are processed, and instructions about when and how to carry over to the next column. It seems very likely that conceptual strategy training for 2- and 3-digit computations will be studied in future work, especially in the light of observations that "expert" teachers teach conceptual strategies for multi-digit operations (e.g., Leinhardt, 1987).

Problem-Solving Strategy Instructional Studies

This section is a review of empirical studies that address strategy instruction in problem solving. Where possible, detailed descriptions of strategies used are provided; in some cases, however, reports were too sketchy to permit anything but a general outline of the strategy.

Peterson, Swing, and Stoiber (1988) trained 15 fourth-grade teachers to teach strategies for solving word problems [*SSR*]. These strategies included defining and describing the problems by providing word definitions, telling what terms in the problem mean, finding the question, identifying problem information, and paraphrasing the problem; comparing, which involves determining similarities and differences between different mathematical operations and problems; thinking of reasons (i. e., justifying problem-solving procedures and answers); and summarizing, defined as putting together the salient features of a problem (e.g. facts, steps, or rules). All four types of strategies were taught to the thinking-skills training group. Illustrations of each strategy are provided in Table 7-5.

Peterson et al. (1988) trained 15 control teachers in effective use of time in the classroom. The recommended procedures included short learning activities, minimizing interruptions, active monitoring during seat work, rules and routines, incentive systems, clear directions, and student behavior management.

Teacher training for both the thinking-skills and control groups included 2 two-hour workshop sessions, feedback sessions, and feedback material. In the treatment group teachers were provided a detailed manual describing the strategies and suggested teaching procedures. The members of the control group were provided with manuals detailing time management skills.

All students were pretested for mathematics achievement in December and posttested the following May after five months of strategy or time-management training in conjunction with regular mathematics instruction. The thinking skills intervention was effective in high-ability classes but not lower-ability classes. However, within classes the high-ability students benefited more from a time intervention than a thinking intervention. Conversely, lower-ability students within these classes tended to benefit more from the thinking-skills intervention. In their interpretation of these results, Peterson et al. suggested that a fairly high level of average math ability is needed to implement thinking skills effectively in a class; however, once the thinking skills treatment is implemented, the lower-ability students within the class seem to benefit most from training. This may be due to the fact that high ability students already use the appropriate thinking skills.

The strategies taught in an earlier study by Charles and Lester (1984) were: paraphrasing problems, drawing diagrams, finding important information, looking for an easier example, making a list or table, using objects, working backwards, checking work, and looking for a pattern across

Table 7-5
Examples of Thinking Skills Strategies

Defining and Describing

Problem:
There are 6 vases. Each vase has 5 flowers in it. How many flowers were used to fill all the vases?

Self-questions:
A good way to start is ask the self-question, *What facts are given? What do they mean?* There are 6 vases. Each one has 5 flowers. *What is a picture that shows this?* The picture should help me answer the question, *What do the facts mean?* My picture says that there are 5 flowers in a group. So there are 6 groups of 5. The question is another fact I have to think about. It says "How many flowers were used to fill the vases?" *What does that mean?* It says *how many* needed to fill *6 vases*. That sounds like I have to find a total. Adding means finding a total. So does multiplying. I already said I have 6 groups of 5. That is exactly what I need to multiply. 6 x 5 = 30.

Comparing

Problem:
Joni bought 9 pencils that each cost 15 cents and 7 erasers that cost 10 cents apiece. How much money did she spend?

Self-questions:
She is buying pencils *and* erasers. How much did she spend? That is what I am trying to find out. I need to find how much money pencils and erasers cost all together. *What math idea do I know that is like that?* What means the same as *all together?* Addition is putting things together to get a total so that would work. You also get a total with multiplication.

problems [SSR]. Twenty-three fifth-grade teachers and 23 seventh-grade teachers participated in the study. Teachers at each grade level were assigned in approximately equal numbers to the thinking strategies condition or to a control condition. Teachers of the treatment classes received three hours of training on the problem-solving program. Control group teachers did not receive any special training. Students were pretested and posttested using two forms of a test measuring problem-solving ability. Twenty-three weeks of regular mathematics instruction, along with strategy instruction for the treatment group, intervened between pretest and

Table 7-5 (cont.)
Examples of Thinking Skills Strategies

Which one should I do? I should think, *How are the operations alike* and different? I already said they are alike because they give a total. *How are they different?* If I add, I write all the numbers down in a column and then add, so I would write 15 cents down 9 times and 10 cents down 7 times. But I could multiply. It is like repreated addition. I can do 15 x 9 and 7 x 10. That is a lot easier. I have to remember to add my two answers together to get a total.

Thinking of Reasons

Problem:
Ben has 125 baseball cards. He traded 32 of them for football cards. How many baseball cards does he have now?

Self-questions:
I think I do it this way: 125 - 32 = 93. My Thinking of Reasons Self-Questions tell me to ask, *Why is this a good way to do the problem?* I think the question wants me to find out how many baseball cards Ben has, not baseball *and* football cards. The problem tells me that Ben has traded 32 baseball cards. So *what are the most important things to remember?* I think there are two things. One is that multiplying is like adding the same number over and over. Second, multiplying is another way of finding how much in all.

From *Learning Time Versus Thinking Skills: Alternative Perspectives on the Effects of Two Instructional Interventions* (1986) by P.L. Peterson, S.R. Swing, and K.C. Stoiber. Madison, Wisconsin: Wisconsin center for Educational Research. Adapted by permission.

posttest. Table 7-6 illustrates the thinking skills prompts provided for the students in the treatment condition.

Strategy training produced improved performance in understanding the problem, developing a plan to solve the problem, and to a lesser extent, in generating the correct result. According to the authors, there are three important benefits of this strategy training. First, the program improves students' willingness to engage in problem solving. Second, the students gained confidence in their ability to succeed in problem solving. Third, the students learn "how to think," as demonstrated by improved understanding of how and when to use strategies, as well as development of common sense and reasoning.

Montague and Bos (1988) provided preliminary evaluation of multiple-strategy training procedure [SSR] with six learning disabled adolescents participating in an uncontrolled pretest-to-posttest study. Training included eight verbal math problem solving strategies. Students were instructed to: (1) read the problem out loud, asking the teacher to pronounce or define any unknown words; (2) paraphrase the problem aloud, stating important information and giving close attention to the numbers in the problems; (3) draw a representation of the problem; (4) state the problem, indicating the known and unknown information; (5) hypothesize, that is, think of a plan to solve the problem; (6) estimate the answer; (7) calculate the answer and show work; and (8) self check, referring to the problem and checking every step to determine accuracy of operations and correctness of response. Training materials included an outline and a wall chart of the strategy, a number of practice problems, and graphs for recording test scores and time taken to complete the tests.

Students were trained in three 50-minute sessions. Their current learning habits were first analyzed. Then the new strategies were described, modelled, verbally rehearsed, and practiced on classroom materials. Throughout strategy acquisition, corrective feedback was provided to each student. Subjects were required to reach a 100% criterion for verbalization of strategy steps from memory. Once criterion was reached, practice in application of strategies was introduced one day before each testing session in order to ensure continued knowledge of the strategies. During testing sessions students were cued to use the strategies. Intervention was discontinued when students achieved an average score of 70% on four consecutive tests. A generalization test, consisting of ten problems of slightly greater difficulty than the training and post-test problems, was administered on the day following the final treatment test.

Due to the small sample size, no statistical analysis was carried out. However, five of the six subjects showed substantial improvement in problem solving after training. Furthermore, four of the six subjects showed some generalization to problems more difficult than those used in training. The time to complete the problem-solving tests increased with treatment, suggesting that subjects were actively employing the strategies.

Hargest et al. (1986) (described earlier) also taught seventh-and eighth-grade students problem solving strategies [SSR]. The strategy training began with instruction in employing a simple formula. For example, in the problem "Find the area of a rectangle that is 6 cm. wide and 7 cm. long. The formula for the area is a = lw, where a is the area, l is the length and w is the width. Solve for a. a = lw. l = 7 cm. w = 6 cm." Students are instructed to follow three steps: (1) Find the formula written in the problem. (2) Put numbers in the formula. (3) Solve.

The second part of instruction involved choosing a reasonable answer for math problems presented in multiple-choice format. The strategy steps

---

Table 7-6
Problem-Solving Guide

Problem Solving

Understanding the Problem
- Read the problem again.
- Write what you know.
- Look for key phrases.
- Find the important information.
- Tell it in your own words.
- Tell what you are trying to find.

Solving the Problem

Try This	Would This Help?
Look for a pattern.	Draw a picture
Guess and check.	Make an organized list or table.
Write an equation.	Use objects or act out the problem.
Use reasoning.	Simplify the problem.
	Work backwards.

Answering the Problem

Have You:
- Used all the important information?
- Checked your work?
- Decided if the answer makes sense?
- Written the answer in a complete sentence?

From "An Evaluation of a Process-Oriented Instructional Program in Mathematical Problem Solving in Grades 5 and 7" (1984) by R.I. Charles and F.K. Lester. *Journal for Research in Mathematics Education, 15,* p. 20. Copyright 1984 by The National Council of Teachers of Mathematics Inc. Reprinted by permission.

---

taught to the students were: (1) Read the problem. (2) Find key words. (3) Decide on an operation. (4) Round off. (5) Solve. (6) Choose the multiple-choice alternative closest to your answer. The rest of the strategy instruction involved specific types of word problems (e.g., money problems using addition and subtraction, making change, problems using percents). The strategies for each of these types of problems included the following steps: (1) Read the problem. (2) Find key words. (3) Decide on operation(s). (4)

Solve. (5) Reread the problem. (6)Evaluate whether the answer is reasonable. The learning strategy intervention improved math problem solving performance.

In a study with students identified as skill deficient in mathematics, Darch, Carnine, and Gersten (1984) taught a number of strategies used to identify the a operation to be used in a word problem [SSR]. Students were instructed: (1) to multiply if you use the same number over and over again, sometimes indicated by the words *each* and *every*; and (2) to check if the "big number" is present in a problem. If so, divide; if not, multiply. Teacher training was conducted over a two-week period with each teacher for the treatment condition using role-playing techniques. There were four treatment groups with two instructional methods evaluated in the context of two different levels of practice. The two instructional treatments were explicit strategy instruction or regular instruction. The students in all groups received eleven 30-minute sessions, consisting of 15 minutes of teacher instruction and 15 minutes of independent seat work on story problem worksheets. The fixed-practice group received no further practice, while the extended-practice group received up to eight extra practice lessons, with the actual number depending on how rapidly students reached criterion accuracy on a problem-solving test.

Subjects were posttested with a 26-item problem-solving test. The explicit strategy group performed significantly better than the regular instruction group; however, there was no effect of extended practice. In a test of maintenance administered ten school days after the original posttest, the group with explicit strategy instruction including extended practice performed better than both the regular instruction groups, although the difference between the two explicit strategy groups was not significant.

Swing and Peterson (1986) conducted a study with 111 grade 5 students as subjects. Students were randomly assigned within classes to a cognitive process group [T], a fact sheet group, and a control group. The cognitive process group received written questions along with word problems. The questions required generation of verbal, pictorial, or procedural problem terms. These questions were designed to promote the integration of definitional and descriptive information in mathematics curriculum material, and to model an elaborative and analytical approach to exercise completion. Table 7-7 provides an example of a problem with processing questions.

Two to four questions preceded one-third of the problems. For the remaining exercises written prompts suggested that students generate their own elaborative questions and respond to them. The fact sheet group were given definitional, procedural, or pictorial representations of the problem terms. For example, if the processing question used the word *perimeter*, the definition of *perimeter* appeared on the fact sheet. Along with the fact sheets, the students received the seatwork problems which made up the core exercises from the cognitive processing worksheets and an additional set of parallel problems. Students in this group studied the fact sheets prior to working on the seatwork problems. The control group received the same problems as the fact sheet group without any added questions or definitions.

Prior to the teaching phase of this study each student had an individual training session lasting from 20 to 40 minutes. Students in the cognitive process group were given a rationale for the use of processing questions, followed by instruction and practice in answering those questions. Students in the fact sheet group were similarly given a rationale for studying the fact sheet, followed by discussion of the importance of conceptual information. Control group participants were informed of the importance of conceptual information. Following the individual training sessions, each group received eight days of mathematics instruction with their respective worksheets.

Students had been pretested for knowledge of mathematical concepts and computational ability. Posttests comprising computational problems, concept questions, story problems, and definition and formula questions were administered immediately following treatment and again two weeks later to test for maintenance.

An examination of seatwork completed by the treatment students revealed that a sizeable number of these subjects completed less than half of the seatwork problems. Those students who were able to complete the majority of the problems were of above average ability. Swing and Peterson

---

Table 7-7
Examples of Worked Problems

The Hills tie their dog Fritz's chain to a stake in the ground and let Fritz run around in circles. The chain is 3 meters long. How far does Fritz run if he runs around the circle once?

1. Think of a picture that shows what the problem is about.

2. What are the key words that tell what to do?

3. What are the key words telling me to do?

4. What facts do I need to use to solve the problem?
What do the facts stand for?

5. Think about the questions and answers for #1, #2, #3, and #4 to help you solve the problem.

From *Elaborative and Integrative Thought Processes in Mathematics Learning* (1986) by S.R. Swing and P.L. Peterson, 1986. Madison, Wisconsin: Wisconsin center for Education Research. Adapted by permission.

argued that the treatment was unlikely to have an effect for those students who did not effectively complete the assigned problems and associated processing questions. This hypothesis was supported since the treatment enhanced performance for the high-ability students but not the low-ability students. Treatment effectiveness was demonstrated by significantly higher computation scores for the high-ability treatment students as compared to the high-ability fact sheet and control students. Furthermore, the high-ability treatment students were significantly better at defining mathematical concepts than their counterparts in the control group. The fact sheet group did not differ significantly from either of the other groups on definitions.

The strategies taught in a study by Lee (1982) [*SSR*] were explicitly adapted from Polya (1957). These strategies included identifying the question, indicating relationships among the items involved in the problem (understanding the problem), drawing a picture, making a chart, looking for special cases and patterns, considering one condition and adding another, looking for similar problems (making a plan), implementing a plan and checking each step (carrying out the plan), determining if the answer obtained was reasonable, finding another way to solve it, and making a similar problem (looking back).

The subjects in this study were 16 average achieving grade 4 students. Subjects could be classified as early or late concrete operational (Piagetian stage classification). The instruction group had 20 problem-solving sessions of approximately 45 minutes each over a period of nine weeks, while the non-instruction group attended regular classes.

The small sample size precluded quantitative analysis; however, there were substantial differences in the number of problems solved by the instruction versus no-instruction groups. On a post-instruction test the strategy instruction group solved an average of 73% of the problems while the non-instructed group only solved 6% correctly. Similarly, in a delayed post-instruction test, four weeks after the end of instruction, the instruction students solved 79% of the problems as compared to 6% for the non-instructed group.

Szetela and Super (1987) conducted a study in which they investigated instruction in problem solving in conjunction with the use of hand-held calculators [*SSR*]. Twenty-four 7th-grade classes participated in the study, which was carried out over one school year. There were three conditions: one included instruction in problem-solving strategies with the use of calculators; a second received instruction in problem-solving strategies without the use of calculators; the third condition consisted of regular mathematics instruction without either problem-solving or calculator instruction. The calculator + problem-solving (CP) teachers and the problem-solving (P) teachers were given two and a half days of instruction on problem-solving strategies. They were also given suggested problems and written guidelines for teaching the strategies throughout the year. Feedback and an opportunity for a discussion was provided several times a year to the

CP and P teachers. The strategies emphasized were the first and fourth steps of Polya's model, and included: 1) guessing, 2) testing, 3) making a systematic list, 4) making a simpler problem, 5) searching for a pattern, and 6) drawing a diagram.

Mid-year tests indicated that the P group scored higher than the control group on several types of problems. In mid-year and end-of-year tests, the CP group performed better than the control group on a problem-solving test for which the solutions required knowledge of the correct operations to use. However, neither problem-solving group performed significantly better than the control group on an end-of-year process problem test which required the use of strategies taught in the P and CP groups. Szetela and Super suggest that the absence of dramatic gains in the problem-solving groups might be attributed to the fact that the problem-solving teachers gave only moderate attention to Polya's four-stage plan. Thus, there might have been some confusion concerning exactly what strategies were to be taught to the students.

A study by Schoen, Friesen, Jarrett and Urbatsch (1981, Experiment 2), focused on instructing students to estimate solutions as part of whole-number computations [SSR]. Four intact classes (two grade 5 and two grade 6) were used in the second study. Students at each grade level were divided into three groups of equivalent ability. The first treatment consisted of two lessons of individual computer-assisted instruction (CAI) drill-and-practice on exact computations of sums, two CAI lessons on exact computations of products, and one review lesson. Each lesson lasted 10 to 15 minutes. Students in the second group received the same lessons except that they were instructed to estimate solutions rather than compute them. Students in the third group completed five worksheets with the aid of hand calculators. The worksheets were designed to present a sequence of lessons leading to an understanding of the use of rounding and estimation. See Table 7-8 for an example of the use of rounding in estimation. Time taken to complete all five worksheets was almost equivalent for the other two groups.

The estimation instruction students were significantly better at quick estimations of word problem solutions on a posttest than either of the other two groups. However, there were no significant differences between the estimation drill-and-practice group and the estimation instruction group on estimating solutions on sums and products, although both of these groups performed significantly better than the computation drill-and-practice group. In a retention test three weeks later the only significant effect was improved performance in the estimation of sums and products for the strategy-instruction group compared to the other groups.

Summary

It is impossible, based on the extant data base, to isolate the individual strategies that are effective in enhancing problem solving. However, a number of strategies recur in the successful interventions. Table 7-9 provides a summary of the strategies taught in each of the studies reviewed, classified under the four stages of Polya's model. Only a few of the studies provide detailed information on how these strategies were implemented and a summary of that information is provided in Table 7-9.

The strategies of reading the problem aloud, paraphrasing, and finding important information fall under the first stage of Polya's model. These strategies were part of successful interventions in a number of studies (e.g., Lee, 1981; Montague & Bos, 1986; Peterson et al., 1986; Swing & Peterson, 1986). It is obvious that strategies pertaining to the first stage are relatively simple and easy to implement. In those studies where instructional process is detailed (e.g., Montague & Bos, 1986; Peterson et al., 1986), students are provided with self-questions to aid in understanding a problem. Thus, they are instructed to ask themselves questions such as "What is being asked?", "What facts are given?", What do the facts mean?", and "What am I looking for?". Not only are these strategies easy to teach, they also seem to be quite effective. In fact, an early study by Stretch (1931) (cited in Hollander, 1973) indicated that instruction in these three strategies plus the injunction to check work (stage four) produced improved problem-solving performance in grade 5 students.

There are three strategies, common to a number of studies, that fall under the stage of devising a plan (Charles & Lester, 1984; Lee, 1982; Montague & Bos, 1986; Szetela & Super, 1987). These three strategies are; drawing a diagram, making a list or table, and looking for an easier example. The strategies of drawing a diagram and making a list or table seem self-explanatory. In fact, the studies which employed drawing a diagram and making a list or table simply informed subjects that these were useful strategies, but did not provide explicit instruction on how to implement

Table 7-8
Rounding as Estimation Strategy

1. Round numbers to some pre-chosen value	7,829 rounds to 8,000 4,220 rounds to 4,000 6,540 rounds to 7,000
2. Perform operation (in this case, addition) on these rounded numbers. The result is the estimate.	8,000 4,000 7,000 ——— 19,000

Table 7-9   Strategies in Studies Reviewed

	Strategy	Peterson et al. (1986)	Charles & Lester (1984)	Montague & Bos (1986)	Hargest et al. (1986)	Swing & Peterson	Lee (1982)	Szetela & Super (1987)	Schoen et al. (1981)
Looking Back	Make a Similar Problem						■		
	Solve Another Way						■		
	Summarize	■							
	Check Answer	■	■	■	■				
	Estimate			■			■	■	■
Devising a Plan	Decide on Operation				■				
	Hypothesize			■					
	Look for a Pattern	■	■				■	■	
	Work Backwards		■						
	Find an Easier Example		■				■	■	
Understanding the Problem	Read Out Loud			■	■				
	Use Objects		■						
	Make a List or Table		■						
	Draw a Diagram		■	■		■	■	■	
	Paraphrase Problem	■		■			■	■	
	Identify Important Information	■	■	■	■				
	Find Question	■				■	■		
	Define Terms	■	■						

Table 7-10
Effective Strategies Identified in the Problem Solving Studies

Problem Stage	Individual Strategy	Operations
Understanding the Problem	Read Out Loud	Ask teacher to prounounce unknown words
	Paraphrase the Problem	State important information, giving close attention to the numbers in the problem
	Finding Important Information	Self Questions: - What is being asked? - What facts are given? - What do they mean? - What am I looking for?
Devising a Plan	Drawing a Diagram	Self Question: - What is a picture that shows this?
	Making a list or table	
	Finding an Easier Example	
Looking Back	Looking for a Pattern Across Problems	Self Questions: - How is this problem like other problems and how is it different? - What else do I know of that is like this?
	Checking Work	
	Estimating Solution	Rounding (See Table 9 for an example of rounding)

them. Perhaps the rationale is that subjects are capable of drawing diagrams and making lists or tables and need only to be reminded of the utility of these procedures. The third suggested strategy of finding an easier example is not as simple to implement. Unfortunately, none of the studies which train this strategy offer details of instruction. For instance, Peterson et al. (1986) provided an example of a student presented with a difficult division problem (5002 divided by 2). When prompted with a self-question "What else do I know about that is like this?", the student generated the simpler problem 5212 divided by 2 and subsequently described the similarities and differences between the two problems. However, Peterson et al. did not provide any information on how to teach children to generate an easier answer. An example provided by Polya (1957) suggests that even with older students generation of an easier example is not a simple process, and in fact requires considerable prompting by the teacher before the student is able to arrive at an easier example (See Table 7-11).

The third stage in Polya's model is carrying out the plan. In the context of word problems, this involves performing the basic computations planned in the second stage. None of the studies that focus on strategies for problem solving include strategies which would fall under carrying out the plan. Thus, the research on strategic training for word problem solutions assumes that the basic mathematical skills are already well developed and do not require any sophisticated strategies beyond those that are routinely taught in the classroom.

Strategies pertaining to the final stage of looking back include looking for a pattern across problems, checking work, and estimating solutions (Charles & Lester, 1984; Montague & Bos, 1986; Peterson et al., 1986; Szetela & Super, 1987). In their detailed instruction manual, Peterson and her colleagues suggest a number of self-questions to encourage a comparison to other problems. These include "What else do I know about that is like this?" and "How is this problem like other problems and how is it different?". The strategy of checking work is not explained in the studies. It would seem that the authors assume that how to instruct this strategy is self-evident. Schoen, Friesen, Jarrett, & Urbatsch (1981, Experiment 1), however, provide explicit information on the instruction of estimation. In their study students were taught to estimate by using rounding, a procedure commonly employed by successful estimators (Levine, 1981; Reys, Rybolt, Bestgen & Wyatt, 1982). Rounding involves choosing new numbers close to the numbers in the original problem in order to make computations simpler. The second step in estimation is computation with these simplified numbers.

Each stage in Polya's model is dependent on effective completion of the preceding stage. For example, unless the problem is understood (stage one), it is impossible to devise an appropriate plan (stage two). In light of this, teachers who wish to employ strategy instruction in problem-solving should address each of the problem-solving stages in the proper order. In fact, it is impossible to attempt any instruction of problem-solving until basic mathematical operations are understood. Once this prerequisite

Table 7-11
Finding an Easier Example

Teacher:	"Do you know a related problem?"
Student:	Silence
Teacher:	"Look at the unknown! Do you know a problem having the same unknown?"
Student:	Silence
Teacher:	"Well, what is the unknown?"
Student:	"The diagonal of a parallelepiped."
Teacher:	"Do you know any problem with the same unknowns?"
Student:	"No. We have not had any problems yet about the diagonal of a parallelepiped."
Teacher:	"Do you know any problem with a similar unknown?"
Student:	Silence
Teacher:	"You see, the diagonal is a segment, the segment of a straight line. Didn't you ever solve a problem whose unknown was the length of a line?"
Student:	"Of course we've solved such problems. For instance, to find a side of a right triangle."
Teacher:	"Good! Here is a problem related to yours and solved before. Could you use it?"

From *How to Solve It* by G. Polya, 1957, Garden city, NY: Doubleday Anchor Books. Copyright 1957 by G. Polya. Reprinted by permission.

knowledge base is attained by students, initial strategy instruction should focus on the first stage of understanding the problem using the strategies described above. Similarly, instruction in devising a plan and looking back should follow in order.

Teacher Strategies

Problem solving can also be affected by the ways teachers present problems [T]. Anand and Ross (1987) trained grade 5 and grade 6 students with personalized, concrete, and abstract problems. Abstract problems involved the use of general referents, such as "fluid" and "quantity." In contrast, concrete problems involved referents that were specific but hypothetical, such as "your teacher" and "candy bar." Finally, personalized problems were those which used personally familiar referents obtained from a biographical questionnaire administered to each student. An example of an abstract problem is: "There are 3 objects. Each is cut in half. In all, how many pieces would there be?" A corresponding concrete problem would be: "Billy had 3 candy bars. He cut each one of them in half. In all, how many pieces of candy bar did Billy have?" A personalized version of the same problem is: "Joseph's teacher, Mrs. Williams, surprised him on December 15th when she presented Joseph with 3 Hershey bars. Joseph cut each one of them in half so that he could share the birthday gift with his friends. In all, how many pieces of Hershey bars did Joseph have for his friends?"

Students in this study performed better on personalized problems than on abstract problems. There were no other significant performance differences. The authors concluded that adapting problem contexts to student interests can increase comprehension as well as improve attitudes toward learning mathematics.

In another study, Caldwell and Golden (1987) supported the conclusion that problems with concrete referents are easier than problems with abstract referents, at least for elementary-school children. However, high school students, who have more practice with abstract concepts, showed no significant performance differences between these two problem types. In addition to the concrete/abstract distinction, Caldwell and Golden also manipulated whether problems were hypothetical or factual. A hypothetical problem describes a situation as well as a possible change in the situation. In contrast, a factual problem merely describes a situation. For example, a concrete hypothetical problem would be: "There are 4 more girls in an English class than boys. If there were 6 times as many girls and twice as many boys, there would be 136 pupils. How many boys are there?" An example of a concrete factual problem is: "A young farmer has 8 more hens than dogs. Since hens have 2 legs each, but dogs have 4 legs each, altogether the animals have 118 legs. How many dogs does the young farmer own?"

The authors found that, at all levels, factual problems are easier than hypothetical problems. In addition, there was a significant interaction between the factual/hypothetical variable and the concrete/abstract variable. Concrete, factual problems were easier for students than concrete, hypothetical problems, while abstract, hypothetical problems were easier than abstract, factual problems. In fact, the greater difficulty of hypothetical problems appears almost exclusively in concrete contexts. Simply stated, students perform best on problems that describe either real situations (concrete/factual) or situations that do not exist (abstract/hypothetical). However, mixing the two depresses problem-solving performance.

De Corte, Verschaffel, and De Win (1985) studied another aspect of problem wording. They compared problems stated in usual textbook form with the same types of problems reworded to make semantic relations between the sets more explicit [T]. Thus, for example, the problem "Joe won 3 marbles. Now he has 5 marbles. How many marbles did Joe have in the beginning?" is reworded to read: "Joe had some marbles. He won 3 more marbles. Now he has 40 marbles. How many marbles did Joe have in the beginning?" In the reworded version, it is explicitly stated that Joe already had some marbles before he won 3 more marbles. The effect of this additional sentence is to identify the unknown start set. Explicitly stating the semantic relations between sets improved problem-solving performance.

Finally, Moyer, Sowder, Threadgill-Sowder and Moyer (1984) compared two different ways of wording problems (normal vs. telegraphic) with presentation in a pictorial format [T]. In the drawn format, the problem was represented by an appropriate picture, with a question indicating the quantity to be calculated. Thus, for example, the picture might contain eight small bags, with the words "bubble gum, 25 pieces, 30 cents" on each bag. The number of bags would be indicated above the picture (e. g. "8 bags"), and the question "How much for eight bags?", printed below the picture, would indicate the quantity to be calculated. The normal verbal version of the above problem read: "There are 8 bags of bubble gum. There are 25 pieces in each bag. Each bag costs 30 cents. How much do the eight bags cost?" The corresponding telegraphic format was: "8 bags of gum. 25 pieces in each bag. Each bag costs 30 cents. How much for 8 bags?"

There was no difference in the difficulty of problems presented in the normal verbal versus the telegraphic format, replicating the results of a previous study by the same authors (Moyer, Moyer, Sowder, & Threadgill-Sowder, 1984). Drawings were associated with better performance for both high- and low-ability readers. Low readers, however, profited more than high readers from the drawn format. The authors suggested that the drawn format may provide additional assistance to the poor readers by removing memory overload due to reading demands in the verbal format.

Based on these studies, it is possible to make some practical suggestions to enhance math performance in elementary-school children. First, presenting problems in pictures can enhance performance, particularly with low-ability students. Second, if problems are presented in verbal format, personalized and concrete problems are easier to solve. Finally, in constructing word problems, teachers can be sensitive to the interaction of referent type (concrete versus abstract) and situation type (hypothetical versus real) reported by Caldwell and Goldin (1987), recognizing that concrete, real problems and hypothetical, abstract problems are easier than the other two types (concrete, hypothetical and abstract, real).

In addition to the study of the effects of the presentation of individual problems, researchers have also addressed the question of how the construction and administration of mathematics tests influence examination performance. Hembree (1980) conducted a meta-analysis of 120 studies on factors other than ability that affect math test achievement, identifying a number of conditions that can enhance performance. Tests constructed with work space located next to the test items and diagrams presented with test problems improve performance [T]. Furthermore, performance on speeded tests is optimal when items are arranged in an easy to to difficult sequence [T]. Students perform better on an open-response tests when scoring allows the opportunity for partial credit [T]. Finally, providing data in the order needed for writing equations markedly improves performance.

Testing conditions also have effects on test performance. Students score higher on tests of problem-solving when feedback about correctness of responses is given item by item during the test [T]. Students appear to learn better in an atmosphere of unannounced testing, and more frequent testing seems to enhance achievement [T]. Hembree also notes that praise delivered at the start of testing enhances performance [T].

Concluding Remarks

In the studies reviewed in this chapter, effective strategy instruction often seems to depend upon explicit training. It is clearly important that teachers know exactly what strategies they are teaching and that they have explicit lesson plans for instruction. It is equally obvious that students must be aware of what the strategies are and when they should be used (Pressley, 1986). In fact, knowledge of strategies is a critical prerequisite to strategy use. For example, in the Montague and Bos study (1986) the researchers spent a major part of the training ensuring that students knew the strategies to use before introducing the application of these strategies. Instructors attempting to teach the strategies outlined in this chapter should be aware of the need to provide their students with organizational and motivational material concerning these strategies.

One caution about strategy instruction. In a number of studies (e.g., Peterson et al., 1986; Swing & Peterson, 1986), there are no overall positive effects for strategy instruction. Rather, the results of instruction seem to depend on the abilities of the students being taught. Strategy instruction is probably more effective with students who lack the trained strategies, although students who lack the necessary prerequisite knowledge will probably not benefit from strategy instruction. Most of the research cited in this chapter does not address the question of aptitude-by-treatment interactions, thus we are unable to recommend the appropriate target populations for each of the strategies considered in this chapter. At this point in time, about all that can be offered is a strong *caveat emptor*, that some students will benefit more from math strategy instruction than others. Nonetheless, the studies reviewed fuel optimism that there are positive effects of strategy instruction for both basic math tasks and more sophisticated problem solving. Teaching the strategies covered in this chapter will benefit at least some students.

REFERENCES

Anand, P.D., & Ross, S.M. (1987). Using computer-assisted instruction to personalize arithmetic materials for elementary school children. *Journal of Educational Psychology, 79*(1), 74-78.

Ashcraft, M.H. (1985). Is it farfetched that some of us remember our arithmetic facts? *Journal for Research in Mathemematics Education, 16*(4), 99-105.

Baroody, A.J. (1985). Mastery of basic number combinations internalization of relationships or facts. *Journal for Research in Mathematics Education, 16*(4), 83-98.

Caldwell, J.H., & Goldin, G.A. (1987). Variables affecting word problem difficulty in secondary school mathematics. *Journal for Research in Mathematics Education, 18*(3), 187-196.

Charles, R.I., & Lester, F.K. (1984). An evaluation of a process-oriented instructional program in mathematical problem solving in grades 5 and 7. *Journal for Research in Mathematics Education, 15* (1), 15-34.

Darch, C., Carnine, D.W., Gersten, R.G. (1984). Explicit instruction in mathematics problem solving. *Journal of Education Research, 77*, 351-359.

Decorte, Vershaffel, L., & DeWin, L. (1985). Influence of rewarding verbal probelms on children's problem representations and solutions. *Journal of Eductional Psychology, 77*, 460-470.

Deshler, D.D., Alley, G.R., Warner, M.W., & Schumaker, J.B. (1981). Instructional practices for promoting skill acquisition and generalization in severely learning disabled adolescents. *Learning Disability Quarterly, 4*, 415-422.

Hargest, J.T., Wood, C., Rose, W.H., & Coughlin, L. (1986) Preparing learning disabled adolescents for a state competency math test. Unpublished manuscript. Bel Air, MD Harford Co MD Public Schools.

Hembree, R. (1987). Effects of noncontext variables on mathematics test performance. *Journal for Research in Mathematics Education, 18*, 197-214.

Hollander, S.K. (1973). Strategies of selected sixth graders reading and working verbal arithmatic problems. (Doctoral diss., Hofstra University, *Diss. Abstr. Int'l.,* 1974, 34, 6258A.

Lee, K.S. (1982). Fourth-graders heuristic problem-solving behavior. *Journal for Research in Mathematics Education, 13,* 110-123.

Leinhardt, G. (1987). Development of an expert explanation: An analysis of a sequence of subtraction lessons. *Cognition and Instruction, 4*(4), 225-282.

Lloyd, J., Saltzman, N.J., & Kauffman, J.M. (1981). Predictable generalization in academic learning as a result of preskills and strategy training. *Learning Disability Quarterly, 4,* 203-216.

Montague, M., & Bos, C.S. (1986). The effect of cognitive strategy training on verbal math problem solving performance of learning disabled adolescents. *Journal of Learning Disabilities, 19*(1), 26-33.

Moyer, J.C., Moyer, M.B., Sowder, L., & Threadgill-Sowder, J. (1984). Story problem formats: Verbal versus telegraphic. *Journal for Research in Mathematics Education, 15,* 64-68.

Moyer, J.C., Sowder, L, Threadgill-Sowder, J., & Moyer, M.B. (1984). Story problem formats: Drawn versus verbal versus telegraphic. *Journal for Research in Mathematics Education, 15*(5), 342-351.

Peterson, P.L., Swing, S.R., & Stoiber, K.C. (1986). *Learning time versus thinking skills: Alternative perspectives on the effects of two instructional methods* (Program Report 86-6). Madison, WI: University of Wisconsin, Wisconsin Center for Education, School of Education.

Polya, G. (1957). *How to solve it* (2nd. ed.). Garden City, NY: Doubleday Anchor Books.

Pressley, M. (1986). The relevance of the good strategy user model to the teaching of mathematics. *Educational Psychologist, 21,* 139-161.

Pressley, M., Borkowski, J.G., & Schneider, W. (1987). Cognitive strategies: Good strategy users coordinate metacognition and knowldege. In K. Vasta & G. Whitehurst (Eds.), *Annals of child development* (Vol. 5, pp. 89-129). Greenwich, CT: JAI Press.

Rathmell, E.C. (1978). Using thinking strategies to teach the basic facts. In M. Suydam & R. Reys (Eds.), *Developing computational skills* (pp. 13-39). Reston, VA: National Council of Teachers of Mathematics.

Reys, R.E., Rybolt, J.F., Bestgen, B.J., & Wyatt, J.W. (1982). Processes used by good computational estimators. *Journal for Research in Mathematics Education, 13*, 183-261.

Reys, R.E., Suydam, M.N., & Lindguist, M.M. (1984). *Helping children learn mathematics.* Englewood Cliffs, NJ: Prentice-Hall.

Rivera, D., & Smith, D.D. (1988). Using a demonstration strategy to teach midschool students with learning disabilities how to compute long division. *Journal of Learning Disabilities, 21*, 77-81.

Schoen, H.L., Friesen, C.D., Jarrett, J.A., and Urbatsch, T.D. (1981). Instruction in estimating solutions of whole number computations. *Journal for Research in Mathematics Education, 12*, 165-178.

Steinberg, R.M. (1985). Instruction on derived facts strategies in addition and subtraction. *Journal for Research in Mathematics Education, 16*(5), 337-355.

Swing, R.S., & Peterson, R.L. (1986). *Elaborative and integrative thought process in mathematics learning* (Program Report 86-5). Madison: University of Wisconson.

Szetela, W., & Super, D. (1987). Calculation and instruction in problem solving in grade seven. *Journal for Research in Mathematics Education, 18*(3), 215-229.

Thornton, C.A. (1978). Emphasizing thinking strategies in basic fact instruction. *Journal for Research in Mathematics Education*, 214-227.

Wood, M., & Dunlap, W.P. (1982). Applications of drill and practice. *Focus on Learning Problems in Mathematics, 4*(2), 15-21.

CHAPTER 8

Getting Started
Teaching Strategies

Our hope is that readers are sufficiently intrigued by this point to want to try strategy instruction in their own classrooms. Perhaps it still seems a little overwhelming. A lot of strategies have been covered in this volume. The first chapter spelled out a rather exacting approach to teaching strategies, one demanding much of the teacher.

We believe most teachers would benefit greatly from formal training in strategy instruction, including supervised practice providing direct explanations (see Chapter 1) about strategies to students. Realistically, however, that is not an option for most teachers, at least in the short term. Thus this chapter, while not intended to substitute for formal instruction, is meant to provide some guidance to those who wish to get started teaching strategies.

We strongly recommend teachers take advantage of courses or workshops on strategy instruction that are available to them. For instance, the Institute for Learning Disabilities at the University of Kansas conducts training institutes across North America, usually contracted by school districts. Should such an opportunity be available, we urge teachers to take it. While the Kansas workshops are directed at special education teachers in particular, many of the general principles covered by the short courses they offer would be of benefit to teachers serving normal populations. In addition, some professional organizations (e. g., the Association for Supervision and Curriculum Development) offer training at various North American sites. A number of teachers have indicated to us that such training was helpful to them as they tried to become strategy instruction professionals.

For the present, we offer five guidelines:

1. Select a Few Strategies to Teach

No child could learn all of the strategies covered in this volume over a short period of time. That is one reason strategy instruction needs to be extended over a number of years of schooling. There are probably strategies appropriate for every level of schooling and probably for all content areas. The teacher new to strategy instruction should take what Pressley, Goodchild, Fleet, Zajchowski, and Evans (1989) call a "small is beautiful" approach, inspired by Schumaker's (1973) approach to economics in the book of that name. Select a few strategies particularly relevant to the students you are teaching and make a commitment to teach these procedures well.

For instance, a teacher may notice her grade 6 students often do not seem to understand thoroughly what they are reading; in particular, they often fail to make appropriate inferences when reading. The teacher would then seek information about reading strategies to promote understanding and integration of text. Chapter 3 of this book can provide a starting point. Representational imagery was one strategy specified in that chapter as promoting construction of coherent representations of text. Teaching children to generate questions about content they read was reviewed as a promising approach to increasing inferential comprehension. Summarization, including constructing paraphrases of material covered in text, was cited as generally benefiting recall of information in text. These strategies would be a good start.

For the beginning strategy instruction teacher, attempting to teach three such strategies is more than enough challenge. Nonetheless, should the starting teacher want more reading strategies, there are other sources to tap. The reference lists for each of the chapters in this volume are good sources for more information, though in many cases these sources are in scholarly journals not always easily accessible. But there are other journals and books available to most teachers to assist them in learning about strategies. Many of the most accessible ones are reviewed briefly in the appendix of this book. We emphasize that not all the strategies specified in these sources have been well validated; many will not have been studied in experiments at all. Thus, care must be exercised in identifying strategies to teach. The books listed in the appendix were selected because they at least make clear whether (and which) strategies recommended in them have been studied by the scientific community. It makes good sense to favor strategies that have proven their worth in well controlled studies, especially if those studies were conducted with students similar to the teacher's own clients.

Why select only validated strategies? Because real dangers follow from instruction of strategies not producing the benefits purported. At a minimum, such strategies are a waste of instructional time. More seriously, they may undermine a teacher's motivation to continue teaching strategies. It is not easy to teach strategies, a theme developed in Chapter 1 and reiterated later in this chapter. If a teacher expends a great deal of effort in teaching strategies with no discernible payoff, she or he will be less likely to continue teaching the same strategy in the future—a good outcome. It is possible, however, the teacher will draw the generalization from one or a few negative experiences with strategy instruction that the entire enterprise is flawed. Even worse, consider the students, particularly weak students who are often prime candidates for strategy instruction. Such students already have low confidence. A teacher leads the child to process according to a strategy presumably capable of producing competent performance. The child has to work quite a bit to learn how to execute most strategies. If such effort—effort expended using what are supposed to be powerful strategies—goes unrewarded, there is the great danger the child may become more convinced than ever that his academic problems really do reflect immutable factors. After all, if learning remains poor for a child using approaches supposedly producing competent performance for most people, an easy inference to draw is that nothing could help this learner (see Borkowski, Rellinger, Carr, & Pressley, in press, for elaboration of this argument). This is not the type of student thinking about "self as learner" teachers want to encourage. Teaching ineffective strategies has the potential for encouraging just such thinking. This danger is more than enough reason to avoid instruction of any strategies other than those already proven effective in believable tests.

Other considerations in selection of strategies:

(a) They should mesh with the rest of the curriculum, being compatible with the goals school is intended to promote. The strategies included in this book were selected largely with this goal in mind.

(b) Strategies teachable with materials already available in the classroom are to be preferred over strategies requiring special merchandise. Most of the strategies covered in this book can be taught with materials commonly found in all present-day schools. Because a number of publishers have offered expensive kits, workbooks, and other resources as part of strategy instruction curricula, many believe strategy instruction to be an expensive component. Keeping it economical is easy as well as fiscally and professionally responsible.

(c) Why is it professional to keep strategy instruction inexpensive from a materials resources point of view? Although buying a kit offered by a publisher seems like an easy way to begin strategy instruction, our general impression is that these should never be adopted *in toto* as provided by the publisher. First, most have never been validated. Second, they may not produce much benefit if used as prescribed, for many are based on an instructional model incompatible with conditions known to enhance strategy instructional efficacy. That is, students are taught a very large number of strategies in a short period of time, with little information provided about where and when to use the approaches and no guidance in applying the strategies across the school day. When strategy instruction has worked, a few strategies were taught at a time, slowly, with plenty of information about specific contexts, and many opportunities to experience guided practice in applying the strategies to important tasks encountered across the school day.

2. Use Powerful Methods of Teaching

Virtually all successful strategy instructors are using a variation on one particular approach to the teaching of strategies. A few strategies are taught at any one time; they are taught well; and they are taught in the context of the ongoing curriculum. Teaching well operationalizes as following the general model of teaching strategies covered in Chapter 1 (see Table 1-2 in that chapter, a good *aide memoire* for this approach to teaching). The model may be more meaningful at this point in the book, given the extensive review of strategies presented in the previous chapters. The teacher *models* the strategy for the students repeatedly, across the school day when opportunities arise. Much of this modeling can be accomplished by the teacher thinking aloud (e.g., Ericsson & Simon, 1983). The teacher provides *extensive explanations* to students about how the strategies can be applied to different tasks encountered at various points in the curriculum. Thus, the teacher electing to instruct imagery, question-generation, and summarization strategies for reading will make a point of letting her students know when she is trying to construct an image of the content covered in the text. She may ask students to try to do so, and have them compare their images with one another. The teacher can provide explanations when student images are errant (e.g., when mixed with fantasy elements neither actually present in the reading nor reasonably inferrable).

The teacher can also overtly construct self-questions as she reads the text, with this activity extended to any text that may be encountered in the course of the school day. For instance, when the school's daily announcement sheet arrives, rather than simply reading the announcements to the class, the teacher can generate thought questions designed to stimulate complete processing of the information in the text. Thus, an announcement such as "The Girl Scouts will sell cookies in the lunch room next week" can prompt several self-questions. The teacher can ask, "Why would the Girl Scouts be selling cookies?" "Why might we want to buy Girl Scout cookies?"

Current events, a staple of many classroom morning exercises, also provides opportunity for the teacher to model self-questioning. Reading an article about athletes using steroids or other drugs can lead the teacher to posit such questions as: "Why is there a lot of attention when athletes use drugs?", "Is there a message here for ordinary boys and girls?", "Since I would have never dreamed X was using drugs, what does that tell me about who else might be using drugs?", "What good might come from an article like this one, which on the face of it seems to be aimed at discrediting prominent people in athletics?"

Teacher modeling and explaining are not enough, however. Frequent and extensive *re-explanations* are absolutely essential, for students usually will misunderstand at least part of the strategy. Good teaching is largely good diagnosing of what it is that students do not understand, followed by explanations focussing on points of difficulty and re-explanations appropriate to the level of understanding of the student. Student practice, with re-explanations by the teacher, continues as long as necessary for the student to acquire the strategic procedure to a high level of confidence. Many strategies take some time to acquire.

Whether students come to value the strategies they are learning, and thus continue to use them after instruction ends depends largely on the students recognizing their performance improves because they are using the strategies in question. Thus, contemporary models of strategy instruction emphasize *students should be taught to monitor their performances*, noting improvements in performance as a function of using the strategy. Sometimes, this improvement is formally plotted by students on graph paper, providing tangible evidence of improvement. Student recognition of gains due to use of strategies is a critical determinant of durable strategy use. It is important for them to come to realize that high performance is not due to immutable ability, uncontrollable luck, or simple effort, but rather effort directed through procedures well matched to the requirements of a task (Borkowski et al., in press; Clifford, 1984).

What is required is more than just continuing to use the procedure; students must appropriately use the strategies they learn. Students need to learn each strategy is appropriate only in certain situations. Thus, a lot of *information should be provided during instruction about when and where to use strategies being acquired; students also should be given many opportunities to practice a new strategy with a range of materials*, both those which can be readily matched to it and those requiring some adjustment of the strategy. Practice with diverse materials permits first-hand opportunities for adapting strategies to new circumstances and learning when the strategy can be adapted and when adaptation will not work. *Students should be taught to size up new assignments before attempting them*, to determine whether they know a procedure that could be used to mediate a task.

In short, strategy instruction is explicit and extensive, with a great deal of supervised student practice and feedback to students from teachers. Teaching is encouragement of generalized strategy use by guiding and reminding students about when and how strategies can be applied to new situations. At first, this process will be difficult for many teachers, but with practice, it will get easier. The only way to learn the types of errors students might make is to work with students; with experience, teachers will recognize errors more quickly, errors they have seen before. Teachers will also build up a repertoire effective for remediating many types of common errors. With practice, it will be more obvious to teachers where strategies being taught can be applied in the curriculum, so they will be in a better position with increasing teaching experience to provide information about where and when to use procedures they are teaching.

3. Motivate Students to Use the Strategies They Are Taught

Students need to understand that success in school and life beyond school are both largely a function of using appropriate strategies. Students should be made aware that the strategies being taught to them are ones used by very good readers, writers, and problem solvers. They are not acquiring mental crutches when they learn strategies, but rather powerful cognitive tools, ones which, in the absence of instruction, are often discovered only by exceptionally good students.

Motivation will be heightened if students are taught strategies that are appropriately challenging. They should not be so difficult to learn that great effort is required to master them. Thus, the imagery, self-generated questioning, and summarizing strategies selected by the teacher are known to be learnable by grade 6 children; they are at an appropriate level of difficulty. They are also strategies promoting learning of content important to grade 6 children, another factor potentially heightening student motivation. Throughout instruction, teachers should emphasize that errors are to be expected and are a natural part of the learning process. In diagnosing student errors in order to make corrective re-explanations, teachers should never make the student feel embarrassed about their mistakes or anxious about their progress. Students should be convinced efforts made to learn strategies are investments, even if success is not immediately apparent. Failure must never be attributed to low ability—doing so could easily undermine future efforts to learn strategies.

In fact, good strategy teaching includes explicit attempts to eliminate such beliefs. For instance, many students with reading difficulties attribute their difficulties to low ability (e.g., "I am dumb"). Such self-concepts should be supplanted by ones more compatible with ideas supporting the learning of strategies. Students should be made aware that their current processing problems are due to their lack of knowledge of the right strategies (e.g., "I could understand this text if I used the right strategy"). Borkowski and his colleagues (Borkowski et al., in press) have provided especially powerful evidence that changing beliefs about the self as a learner as part of strategy instruction can have a profound effect on the success of strategy instruction. What is most apparent from that research is that students' motivation to use strategies they are learning can be heightened dramatically if they come to believe they are capable of acquiring strategies improving performance, if they begin to think acquisition of such procedures is a more powerful determinant of performance than innate abilities.

The motivational recommendations in this subsection are all very contemporary, emerging from research undertaken in the last five years. Many old ideas about motivation should not be ignored in designing strategy instruction, however. Students can be offered incentives and rewards for acquiring strategies. Praise should be provided throughout the process. The long-term advantages of learning strategies can be highlighted as well. Students can be reminded of the economic, social, and personal advantages accruing from effective comprehension of what is read. For instance, one school emphasizing problem-solving strategies arranges for visits from engineers, scientists, and local businessmen who inform students of the importance of mathematics and problem solving in their professional lives.

4. Encourage Students to Believe They Can Become Good Information Processors

Students should be encouraged to believe they can grow up to be like engineers, scientists, and community business leaders—that is, effective thinkers fulfilling important roles in their community. It is important for students to understand that such roles are not achieved on the basis of innate ability, but rather on the basis of learning the strategies and knowledge associated with these roles. Thus, lawyers know many lawyering strategies, physicians strategies for producing particular medical outcomes, and urban planners tactics for accomplishing striking changes in ever-changing cities. These professionals did not always know how to do these things. They learned the tactics of their profession in school. Most critically, when they were in grade 6, they were much like today's grade 6 students. Students should be encouraged to recognize that they could become like these leaders, and that a good start in pursuit of this role is to learn the academic strategies used by successful people—to acquire the reading, writing, and problem-solving strategies these people know. Make it clear to them many adults do not have these skills and lack of such skills can be a cause of adult failure. Learning important academic skills is something a grade 6 student can do to increase the odds of later success.

In short, it is important for students to believe it possible for them to become good strategy users and that becoming a good strategy user is an important part of developing into an effective participant in society. Believing in a possible self better than the current self can have important motivational consequences. A possible self can provide "direction and impetus for action, change, and development" (Markus & Nurius, 1986, p. 960). It can motivate learning to reduce the difference between the current self and the desired possible self. Who does not know a child who has set his sight on a long-term career goal, with much energy directed toward achieving that goal? An important part of strategy instructional education is to encourage students' understanding that acquisition of academic strategies can reduce the distance between their current selves and the possible selves to which they aspire.

Perhaps a little more concretely, students can be made aware of how the strategies they are learning in school can mediate many real-life demands. Brophy (198a) provides a nice summary of this idea:

> Basic language arts and mathematics skills are used daily when shopping, banking, driving, reading instructions for using some product, paying bills and carrying on business correspondence, and planning home maintenance projects or family vacations....In general, a good working knowledge of the information, principles, and skills taught in school prepares people to make well-informed decisions that result

in saving time, trouble, expense, or even lives, and it empowers people by preparing them to recognize and take advantage of the opportunities that society offers....Do what you can to rekindle this appreciation in your students by helping them to see academic activities as enabling opportunities to be valued (p. 30).

In short, students should be taught they are capable of acquiring strategies important in the real world. Much of the role of education is to pass on strategies of great ecological validity. What is being taught in school is relevant now and in the future.

5. Following Initial Success in Teaching Strategies, Extend the Approach in the Curriculum

Suppose the teacher tries teaching imagery, question-generation, and summarizing strategies, and all goes well. He or she should be in a better position to continue teaching those same procedures the next year, for a lot of knowledge about students' reactions to such instruction will be acquired during the initial year of teaching. The teacher will have acquired a repertoire of routines for responding to common errors made by students in attempting to use strategies.

In addition to continuing instruction of the three reading strategies, there may be other curricula areas in need of instructional enrichment. Typically, grade 6 students are expected to begin learning how to construct coherent essays, and are often not very good at it. The teacher might want to try instruction of strategies for improving qualitative aspects of writing. Some of the writing strategies outlined in Chapter 6 could be attempted, using the teaching sequence specified earlier in this chapter and reviewed more generally in Chapter 1. Because such writing strategies require instruction over a long period of time, the plan might be to practice them throughout the year whenever students are given an essay assignment.

Teachers experiencing success with strategy instruction in their own classrooms can often provide valuable information to teaching colleagues. In particular, a grade 6 teacher can provide information to grade 7 teachers about strategies taught in grade 6, and thus stimulate discussion about how the grade 7 teachers might build upon and add to what has already been taught.

There are now quite a few schools across North America in which a number of teachers provide strategy instruction. Visits to some of them have confirmed that these teachers have a sense that they are on the cutting edge, providing instruction consonant with recommendations in the most modern curriculum outlets. This book was motivated in part by communications from these teachers that any resource providing information about well-validated strategies would be professionally useful to them. We hope that will be the case with this book.

REFERENCES

Borkowski, J.G., Carr, M., Rellinger, R., & Pressley, M. The dependence of self-regulated strategy use on attributional beliefs, self-esteem, and metacognition. In B.F. Jones & L. Idol (Eds.), *Dimensions of thinking: Review of research*. Hillsdale, NJ: Lawrence Erlbaum & Associates.

Brophy, J. (1986). *On motivating students* (Occasional Paper No. 101). East Lansing: Institute for Research on Teaching, Michigan State University.

Clifford, M.A. (1984). Thoughts on a theory of constructive failure. *Educational Psychologist, 19*, 108-120.

Ericsson, A., & Simon, H.A. (1983). *Verbal protocol analysis*. Cambridge MA: MIT Press.

Markus, H., & Nurius, P. (1986). Possible selves. *American Psychologist, 41*, 954-969.

Pressley, M., Goodchild, F., Fleet, J., Zajchowski, R., & Evans, E.D. (1989). The challenges of classroom strategy instruction. *Elementary School Journal, 89*, 301-342.

Schumaker, E.F. (1973). *Small is beautiful: Economics as if people mattered*. London: Blood & Briggs.

Additional Sources of Information about Strategy Instruction

All of the following sources are recommended for teachers who want more information about strategies. $\underline{A}$ journals tend to carry articles about how to teach particular strategies; $\underline{B}$ journals publish formal reports of research on cognitive strategies; $\underline{C}$ lists recommended books that provide information about how to teach many strategies and summaries of relevant research data; and $\underline{D}$ lists books produced by Pressley and his associates which summarize the available scientific evidence supporting strategy training.

There is a caveat attached to the recommendation to rely on these sources for more information about strategies. None of the $\underline{A}$ sources or the $\underline{C}$ texts are based exclusively on strategies that have been validated in formal studies. Therefore, care must be exercised in accepting the recommendations in these sources.

Journals

A. Readily available to teachers, generally written for nonresearcher professionals, and regularly publishing articles about strategy instruction:
Arithmetic Teacher
Educational Leadership
Elementary School Journal
Journal of Learning Disabilities
Journal of Reading
Learning Disabilities Quarterly
Reading Teacher
Remedial and Special Education
Teaching Exceptional Children

B. More written for researcher professionals:
American Educational Research Journal

Cognition and Instruction
Journal of Educational Psychology
Journal of Reading Behavior
Journal of Research in Mathematics Education
Review of Educational Research
Reading Research Quarterly

C. Textbooks

Baroody, A. J. (1987). *Children's mathematical thinking*. New York: Teacher's College Press. The best summary of information processing-inspired mathematics instruction, with substantial commentary on theory and research provided throughout.

Devine, T. G. (1987). *Teaching study skills: A guide for teachers*. New York: Allyn & Bacon. Good source of information about strategies, although emphasis is on strategies for high school and university students. Coverage includes all major contents in the curriculum, plus writing of term papers, class notetaking, memory, and motivation.

Duffy, G.G., & Roehler, L.R. (1989). *Improving classroom reading instruction: A decision-making-approach*. New York: Random House. Covers all aspects of reading instruction, with detailed coverage of how many reading skills can be taught as strategies.

Flower, L.S. (1989). *Problem-solving strategies for writing*. New York: Harcourt Brace Jovanovich. Although intended primarily as a university freshmen-level composition text, the information-processing model of composition can be appropriately adapted to teaching younger children how to write.

Gagné, E.D. (1985). *The cognitive psychology of school learning*. Boston: Little, Brown. An excellent textbook on the cognitive approach to instruction. Covers all of the major content areas of the elementary-school curriculum.

Mayer, R.E. (1987). *Educational psychology: A cognitive approach*. Boston: Little, Brown. Another excellent textbook on cognitive approaches to teaching. Coverage similar to Gagné, although a little broader and more current.

McNeil, J.D. (1987). *Reading comprehension* (2nd edition). Glenview, IL: Scott, Foresman. The best short summary of reading comprehension strategies available. Used in many reading clinics. Very appealing because of nice expositions of the strategies, with readable commentaries about research support for strategies covered.

Tierney, R.J., Readence, J.E., & Dishner, E.K. (1985). *Reading strategies and practices: Guide for improving instruction*. Boston: Allyn & Bacon. An excellent source book for all aspects of the reading process. A great strength of this volume is its summaries of a great deal of research supporting recommendations made.

D. Other books by Pressley and his associates.

McCormick, C.B., Miller, G.E., & Pressley, M. (1989). *Cognitive strategy instruction: From basic research to educational applications*. New York & Berlin: Springer-Verlag. An up-to-date, state-of-the-art summary of cutting edge research on cognitive strategy instruction.

Pressley, M., & Levin, J.R. (Eds.) (1983). *Cognitive strategy training: Educational applications and theoretical foundations*. New York & Berlin: Springer-Verlag. This two-volume set summarizes most of the important research on cognitive strategies conducted as of 1983.

Author Index

Subject Index

U-V-W-X-Y-Z